W9-BOM-562

# THE HEALING
# POWER OF
# MIND

*Tulku Thondup*

# THE HEALING POWER OF MIND

SIMPLE MEDITATION EXERCISES
FOR HEALTH, WELL-BEING,
AND ENLIGHTENMENT

*Foreword by Daniel Goleman*

SHAMBHALA
BOSTON & LONDON
1996

Shambhala Publications, Inc.
Horticultural Hall
300 Massachusetts Avenue
Boston, Massachusetts 02115

© 1996 by Tulku Thondup Rinpoche

Buddhayana Series VII

The calligraphy on page 190 is by Chögyam Trungpa Rinpoche.

9  8  7  6  5  4  3  2

Printed in the United States of America

⊗ This edition is printed on acid-free paper that meets
the American National Standards Institute Z39.48 Standard.

Distributed in the United States by Random House, Inc.,
and in Canada by Random House of Canada Ltd.

*Library of Congress Cataloging-in-Publication Data*
Thondup, Tulku.
    The healing power of mind: simple meditation
    exercises for health, well-being, and enlightment /
    by Tulku Thondup: foreword by Daniel Goleman.
        p.   cm.
    Includes bibliographical references and index.
    ISBN 1-57062-239-6 (alk. paper)
        1. Spiritual life—Buddhism.   2. Health—
    Religious aspects—Buddhism.   3. Spiritual healing.
    I. Title.
    BQ7805.T46   1996        96-6922
    294.3′4446—dc20          CIP

# CONTENTS ~

# FOREWORD ～

## *by Daniel Goleman*

AMONG THE more profound accomplishments of modern science has been the discovery that mind and body are not separate
and independent, but rather the same entity seen from two different angles. Descartes, in setting mind and body apart, was mistaken. And Western medicine, in following his lead, has been
equally wrong in discounting the significance of patients' mental
states for their physical condition.

One sign of the strength of the connection between mind
and body is the finding, in an analysis of more than one hundred
studies linking emotions and health, that people who are chronically distressed—whether anxious and worried, depressed and
pessimistic, or angry and hostile—have double the average risk of
getting a major disease in the ensuing years. Smoking increases
the risk of serious disease by 60 percent; chronic emotional distress by 100 percent. This makes distressing emotion almost double the health risk compared with smoking.

Researchers in the new scientific field of psychoneuroim-
munology, which studies the biological links between mind,
brain, and the immune system, are rapidly filling in the missing
mechanisms that connect mind and body. The emotional centers

of the brain, they are discovering, are tightly linked not just to the immune system, but also to the cardiovascular system. When we are chronically stressed—when the body is continually catapulted into the "fight-or-flight" response, with its surging stress hormones—it weakens the immune system's ability to fight off viruses and nip budding cancers, even as it primes the heart to escalate blood pressure and pump more frantically to prepare the body for emergency. The end result is that our vulnerability to diseases of every category is increased.

By contrast, a mind at peace with itself protects the body's health. That principle is fundamental in traditional Tibetan medicine, an ancient system that has never lost sight of the crucial link between mind and body.

Tulku Thondup, an adept of the Nyingma branch of Tibetan Buddhism, has distilled for Westerners the soul of his culture's approach to health—not just of body and mind, but of spirit as well. As he makes clear, the three are inextricably connected. To the degree that we can "loosen the tightness of grasping"—that is, to the degree we can drop the small and large preoccupations that limit and constrain our vision—and instead relax into a larger, more spacious sense of ourselves and our place in the universe, to that degree we can marshal the healing power of mind.

Tulku Thondup offers us more than a theoretical framework for approaching health: he gives us practical methods, proven over the centuries in Tibetan practice. And in doing so he outlines a means toward healing not just the body, mind, and spirit, but the heart as well. As such, this healing path is a spiritual practice, a way to transform our very lives.

# ACKNOWLEDGMENTS ～

I AM THANKFUL to Harold Talbott for his wisdom, care, and perseverance in editing this book and to Robert Garrett for making this book widely accessible with his mastery in the art of editing. My gratitude goes to Emily Hilburn Sell for shaping the book into its present form with her professional insight and to Ian Baldwin for his invaluable editorial contributions and tireless expert guidance. I thank Daniel Goldman for kindly providing the illuminating foreword to the book.

I am thankful to Lydia Segal for helping in many stages of my research and writing; to Amy Hertz, Jonathan Miller, and Brian Boland for their valuable suggestions; to David Dvore for computer assistance; and to the private Library of Kyabje Dodrupchen Rinpoche at the Mahasiddha Nyingmapa Temple and the Lehman Library at Columbia University for their indispensable resources, and to Victor and Ruby Lam for allowing me to work in their cozy apartment.

I am highly grateful to Michael Baldwin for keeping the lights of our projects on with his tireless guidance and infinite inspiration and to the members and patrons of Buddhayana, under whose most generous sponsorship I have been given the opportunity to work on my research and writing for the last fifteen years.

Finally, my gratitude is due to Samuel Bercholz and the staff of Shambhala Publications for their great care in providing the perfect channel for this book, including Kendra Crossen for refining the book with her superb editorial skills and enthusiasm.

*Acknowledgments*

xiv

# THE HEALING
# POWER OF
# MIND

# INTRODUCTION

I was born into a humble nomad family in a tent on the wild green, grassy tablelands of Eastern Tibet, among the world's highest mountains and biggest rivers. The land was covered with snow for almost eight months of the year. My family belonged to a tribal group that lived in tents, tending many domestic animals including yaks, horses, and sheep. Many times a year we used to move our camps to different valleys, so that there would be enough fresh grass for the animals to live on.

At the age of five, a drastic change shook my life. I was recognized as a reincarnation of a celebrated religious master of Dodrupchen monastery, an important learning institution in Eastern Tibet. Buddhists accept the principle of rebirth and karma, so Tibetans believe that when a great master dies, he or she will take rebirth as a person who will have great ability to benefit people. Because I was their only child, my parents were very sad to give me up, yet they offered me to the monastery without hesitation. My parents were proud and felt deeply privileged that their child had become one of the respected persons in their valley overnight.

Suddenly every aspect of my life changed. I didn't have a so-called normal childhood of playing with other children. Instead, dignified tutors took care of me and served me with respect, for

I had been recognized as the reincarnation of their teacher. I felt at home with my new life, as children always find it easier than adults to adapt to new situations. I loved my parents, especially my grandmother, but told them not to enter the monastery, although they had been given a special temporary permit. People took this as another sign that I had lived in the monastery in my previous life.

From dawn to dusk, the cycle of time was filled with learning and prayer. In this environment, most of the time I was filled with inner joy and peace. My tutors were very compassionate, understanding, and practical people. They were not rigid-minded disciplinarian monks, as you might imagine, although that could sometimes be the case. Instead they were gentle, humble, and caring human beings full of joy and smiles. After some time I did not feel the urge to play or move around without purpose. I did not even feel the need to look around much, and could sit still for hours. First I took the vow of a novice and then of a monk. My hair was shaved every month or so, and after midday we didn't eat anything till the next morning. Our days were regulated by the cycles of the moon and sun. Until the age of eighteen, I never saw an airplane or an automobile. A wristwatch may have been the most sophisticated product of modern technology that I ever came across before leaving the monastery.

For us, Buddhism was not just meditation, study, or ceremony but a way of daily life and existence. Buddhism teaches that the essential identity of all beings is the mind, which in its true nature is pure, peaceful, and perfect. It is the Buddha. As we know, when our mind remains free from the pressure of external situations and emotions, it becomes more peaceful, open, wise, and spacious.

In the monastery I was taught the importance of loosening the attitude that Buddhists call "grasping at self." It is the mistaken perception of a solid, permanent entity in oneself and in other beings or things. "Self" is a concept fabricated by ordinary mind, not by the mind in its true nature. Grasping at self is the root of mental and emotional turmoil, the cause of our suffering. This is the point at which we can understand the very heart of Buddhism, its spirit and its flavor. Do you see how radical Buddhism is? For Buddhism says that suffering is caused by something that our mind is doing even before we reach the point of any unskillful or problematic behavior or any divisive speech, before we are launched into the suffering, sickness, old age, and death that are the career of all living beings. In Buddhism all the trouble is traced to, is pinned on grasping at self. A great Buddhist master named Shantideva portrayed the self at which we grasp as the "evil monster":

All the violence, fear, and suffering
That exists in the world
Comes from grasping at self.
What use is this great evil monster to you?
If you do not let go of the self,
There will never be an end to your suffering.
Just as, if you do not release a flame from your hand,
You can't stop it from burning your hand.

But how can we let go of the self? For me, realization of my true nature wasn't possible at such a young age and so early a stage of my training. But as I progressed through different degrees of physical and mental discipline, I was inspired by and inspirited with mindfulness, compassion, devotion, contemplation, and pure perception. That resulted in progressive degrees of the loosening of my mental and emotional grip of grasping at self and my harvesting more inner strength, awareness, and openness. As my mind was gradually introduced to its peaceful nature and I trained myself to relax in it, the turmoil of external circumstances began to have less impact on my feelings and became easier to handle. The experiences of the peaceful and open nature of the mind enabled me to heal the harsh events of my life and maintain strength and joy in both good and bad circumstances.

At the age of eighteen, because of the political changes in Tibet, accompanied by my two teachers and eight other friends, I had to travel for many months, trekking over a thousand miles across Tibet to escape into India. Halfway, at a holy cave in an empty valley, where high gray mountains stood watch in every direction, Kyala Khenpo, my teacher, who had looked after me like my sole parent since I was five, breathed his last breath. Suddenly I realized that I was an orphan, an escapee, and a homeless refugee.

Finally we arrived in India, a land rich in wisdom and civilization. For the first time in many months I was able to enjoy the feeling of coolness in the shade of trees and ease in the warmth of shelters. Many of the Tibetan refugees in India, who numbered about one hundred thousand, died because of the changes of food, water, weather, or altitude. For those who survived, the painful lives of our loved ones whom we left behind in Tibet kept haunting us day and night.

In those dark days, all I had to guide and console me was the wisdom light of Buddhism in my heart. If a problem could be solved and was worthy of being attended to, I tried to dedicate my life to solving it with a peaceful mind, open attitude, and joyful disposition. If the problem was insoluble, I tried not to burn myself and waste my time and energy in vain. In either situation, I tried to let go of the emotions, the fixations of the mind, by not grasping at them, dwelling on them, or worrying about them, for that would only worsen the situation. Shantideva says:

> If you can solve your problem,
> Then what is the need of worrying?
> If you cannot solve it,
> Then what is the use of worrying?

Ever since my escape to India, I have not lived in a monastic community or observed monastic disciplines. But the peaceful and joyful images of my monastic sanctuary in Tibet are still vivid in my mind's eye. The echoes of the kind, soothing words of the supremely wise and compassionate teachers of my childhood still ring in my ears. More important, the experience of openness, peace, and strength that I cultivated then has been refined and brightened in my heart by the hardships that I faced in my life, just as gold is refined by melting and beating it. Those images, words, and experiences have always been the guiding light and healing energy through the pain, confusion, and weaknesses of my life.

Sheltering the candlelight of a peaceful mind from the storm of life's struggles, and sending out the rays of openness and positive attitude in order to reach others, were the two factors that enabled me to carry on through difficult times. In many ways, the great tragedies of my life turned out to be blessings: They illustrated the Buddhist teachings on the illusory nature of life, stripping away the false security blanket. No doubts were left about the healing power of releasing the grip of grasping at self.

In 1980 I moved to the United States, the land of freedom and abundance. Generally, it is harder for the peaceful mind to survive the assaults of sensual joy and material attraction than those of pain and suffering. But the effect of Buddhist trainings is that, while I enjoy the material prosperity of the West, I appreciate that much more the humble, earthy, and natural Buddhist life of my childhood. Also, the more I enjoy my spiritual life in Buddhism, the more I appreciate the faith, compassion, and generosity based on Judeo-Christian values combined with the material prosperity of the West, which in turn have enriched my spiritual strength. Living in the light of Buddhist wisdom, I view the positive qualities of every circumstance through the window of the peaceful nature of mind instead of succumbing to the negative qualities. This is the heart of the path of healing.

In 1984, I was able to visit Tibet, my homeland, for the first time in twenty-seven years. It was a time of joy to see a few of my old friends and relatives who had survived and a time of sadness to learn that most of my loved ones, whose faces I had been cherishing in memory for years, and my respected teachers, whose words were the source of my healing, had perished. The monastery, the learning institution of my memory, had remained silent for decades with its broken walls. Recently a number of monks have started to return to rebuild the monastery and their monastic lives.

Most of them were able to accept and to heal from their unfortunate experiences without needing to blame somebody else. It is true that one can temporarily feel good by blaming one's misfortunes on others, but this always ends up causing greater pain and confusion. Accepting without blame is the true turning point of healing. It is the healing power of mind. That is why Shantideva writes:

> Even if you cannot generate compassion
> Toward those who are forced to harm you
> Because of their emotional afflictions [of ignorance and anger],
> The last thing you should do is to become angry with them.

In Tibet people go to religious teachers for spiritual teachings and blessings or to ask for prayers to heal their problems or achieve their mundane or spiritual goals. Rarely do they go for consultation about their psychological, social, or physical problems. However, in Western culture, clergy people are consulted about all kinds of life problems. Since my arrival in the States, whenever friends encountered difficulties, they came to me for advice. To my amazement, I was able to suggest healing solutions for many of their problems. The secret wasn't that I was equipped with any therapeutic skill, healing art, or mystical power, but that I have trained myself in the wisdom of Buddhism and have gained skill in healing the painful circumstances of my own life. That discovery inspired me to present Buddhist views and trainings on healing in the form of a book.

This book is a practical guide for anyone wishing to find peace and to heal worry, stress, and pain. It is a compendium of teachings on the wisdom of healing that I have learned from the holy scriptures of Buddhism and have heard from the soothing voices of great masters. This wisdom became the most powerful source of healing for me and for many friends of mine. These are Buddhism's teachings on healing, and I am merely attempting to bring them to you, without overshadowing them with my own voice and idea.

The book has three parts. The first is an overview of every-day living and meditation, the necessary ingredients for healing. The second part presents specific exercises for healing mental, emotional, social, and spiritual problems. Physical problems are the hardest to heal, but they, too, can often be helped by exercises that generate peace, strength, and positive energy, the ultimate fount of our physical well-being. The final section presents several Buddhist meditations that are concerned not only with everyday problems but also with awakening the presence of Buddha qualities that we all possess and with opening the infinite healing power of the Buddha Mind for ourselves and others.

The guidance and advice in this book is derived from Buddhist teachings, especially from a short but unique text entitled *Turning Happiness and Suffering into the Path of Enlightenment*, by Dodrupchen, Jigme Tenpe Nyima (1865–1926), one of the leading lamas and authoritative scholars of the Nyingma school of Tibetan Buddhism, and from other texts such as *A Guide to the Bodhisattva's Way of Life* by Shantideva (eighth century), one of the great Indian masters of Mahayana Buddhism.

Above all, whatever words of healing wisdom are found in these pages are inspired by the kindest and wisest person I ever met in human flesh, my gracious teacher Kyala Khenpo Chöchog (1892–1957). In his care I was nourished for fourteen years like a son by his father. If any errors have crept into the book, they are the indulgences of my own ignorant mind, and for these it is my spiritual obligation to pray for forgiveness from all enlightened masters and compassionate readers.

If you follow the exercises given in this book, you could heal your pain and problems and restore joy and health to your life. At the very least, they will help you reduce the degree of your pain and problems, while increasing joy and health. Moreover, the peace and strength produced by the healing power of mind will equip you to accept pain and problems with greater ease, as just a part of life, much as we welcome the darkness of night as a part of the cycle of the day.

I hope this book will help people learn how to be happier and healthier. Any person whose mind is open to the healing power will benefit by following the healing exercises in this book. There is no need to be a so-called Buddhist. However, the exercises are not meant as alternatives to conventional treatment. Proper medicine, behavior, diet, and exercise are always essential for healing.

PART ONE

# THE
# HEALING
# PATH

# 1

# FOUNDATIONS OF HEALING ~~~

OUR MINDS possess the power of healing pain and creating joy. If we use that power along with proper living, a positive attitude, and meditation, we can heal not only our mental and emotional afflictions, but even physical problems.

When we cling to our wants and worries with all our energy, we create only stress and exhaustion. By loosening the attitude that Buddhists call "grasping at self," we can open to our true nature, which is peaceful and enlightened. This book is an invitation to the awakening of our inner wisdom, a source of healing we all possess. Like a door opening to this wisdom, we can bring in the sunlight, warmth, and gentle breeze of healing. The source of this energy is ours to touch and share at any moment, a universal birthright that can bring us joy even in a world of suffering and ceaseless change.

In Buddhism, the wisdom taught in the scriptures is mainly aimed at realizing enlightenment. However, spiritual exercises can also help us find happiness and health in our everyday life. There are extensive discourses in Buddhism on improving our ordinary life and having a peaceful, joyous, and beneficial existence in this very world.

Buddhism advocates releasing the unnecessary and unhealthy tension that we create in our lives by realizing the truth of how things really are. I have seen many examples of the healing power of the mind for mental and emotional problems, and for physical sickness too.

One example is from my own life. When I was eighteen, my dear teacher Kyala Khenpo and I decided to flee Tibet because of political turmoil, knowing that we were losing home, country, friends, and livelihood. In an empty but sacred valley, Kyala Khenpo died from old age and sickness. He was not only my kind and enlightened teacher, but had cared for me as a parent since I was five. This was one of the saddest and most confused times of my life. However, my understanding of impermanence—the fact that everything always changes in life—made it easier to accept. Spiritual experiences enabled me to remain calm, and the wisdom lights of teachings made the path of my future life clearer to me. In other words, recognizing the nature of what was happening, opening to it, and using sources of power that I had already been given helped me heal from my loss more easily. As we shall see, these three basic steps—acknowledging difficulties and suffering, opening to them, and cultivating a positive attitude—are integral to the healing process.

Another of my teachers, Pushul Lama, had mental problems throughout his youth. He was so destructive that when he was a teenager, his family had to tie him up to protect others—and himself—from his violence. Through healing meditations— mainly of compassion—he healed himself and later became a great scholar and teacher. Today I know of no person more cheerful, peaceful, and kind.

When I lived in Tibet, physical healing through meditation and the right attitude were a common part of everyday life. So now when people ask me for examples of physical healing, it's not easy to figure out which story to tell. For someone from Tibet, it is accepted as an ordinary event that the mind can heal the body. The mind leads the energies of the body—this is how it is. There were so many healings, I never paid much attention when I was younger. However, I do know of one recent example that many people might find amazing, even if it is not very surprising from the Buddhist point of view.

A couple years ago, the present Dodrupchen Rinpoche, a highly spiritual living lama, had an attack of severe appendicitis while traveling in the remote countryside of Bhutan. A senior minister of the country arranged for a helicopter to take him to a hospital. The doctors were afraid Rinpoche's appendix would rupture, and the pain was very great. Against the strong advice of his doctors, he refused surgery and healed himself using meditations and mantras.

## ANYONE CAN BENEFIT

The ability to recover from such a serious sickness through meditation depends on a person's level of trust and spiritual experience. Of course, most of us would be very glad to have the opportunity for surgery if our appendix were about to burst! I only tell this true story to illustrate the power of the mind, and because people have such a strong interest in maintaining their physical health. Few of us are spiritual masters. But anyone can benefit from meditation and a positive attitude. Beginning from where we are right now, it is possible to live a happier and healthier life.

Although physical sickness is one subject you will read about here, this book is meant mostly as a manual for dealing with our everyday emotions. This is the best starting place for most of us. If we can learn to bring greater contentment into everything we do, other blessings will naturally flow.

The views and meditation exercises in this book are inspired mainly by teachings of Nyingma Buddhism, the oldest school of

Buddhism in Tibet, dating to the ninth century, a school that combines the three major Buddhist traditions: Hinayana, Mahayana, and Vajrayana. However, you need not be a Buddhist to use this book. Unfortunately, many people perceive Buddhism as a religion propagated by a particular historical teacher, the Shakyamuni Buddha, that is intended to benefit only the followers of this tradition.

Buddhism is a universal path. Its aim is to realize universal truth, the fully enlightened state, Buddhahood. According to Shakyamuni Buddha himself, an infinite number of beings realized Buddhahood before he was born. There are, were, and will be Buddhism, the path, and Buddhas (those who have realized enlightenment) in this world as well as other worlds, in the past, present, and future. It is true that almost twenty-five hundred years ago, Shakyamuni Buddha propagated teachings that became known as Buddhism. The Buddhism taught by Shakyamuni is one of the appearances of Buddhism, but it is not the only one. People whose minds are open will hear the true way, which Buddhists call Dharma, even from nature. The *Dharmasamgiti* says: "People who have mental well-being, even if the Buddha is not present, will hear Dharma from the sky, walls, and trees. For seekers whose minds are pure, teachings and instructions will appear just by their own wishes."

Buddhism recognizes the differences in cultures and practices of people around the world, and in individual upbringings and personalities. Many other cultures and religions have traditions of healing, and offer specific advice about suffering. Even in Tibet there are many approaches to Buddhism. Having different approaches is good, even if they sometimes appear to contradict one another, because people are different. The whole purpose is to suit the needs of the individual.

## MEDITATION, MIND, AND BODY

Healing through meditation is not limited to a particular religious belief. Nowadays, many physicians trained in conventional

Western medical science are recommending traditional methods of meditation as a way to restore and maintain mental and physical health. These practices rarely acknowledge the experience of what Buddhists call the true nature or the great openness, but instead emphasize visualization and the development of a positive attitude and positive energy. High blood pressure, which in many cases is created and aggravated by mental stress, is particularly responsive to such alternative treatments. Some physicians recommend concentrating the mind on a physical point where the muscles are contracted and then consciously releasing those muscles, so that relief and relaxation will result. This technique follows the same principle as the Buddhist way of recognizing a problem and loosening the grasping at it.

Healing is most effective if it is accompanied by any spiritual belief or meditation experience. Herbert Benson, M.D., of Harvard Medical School, who originated the Relaxation Response, writes: "If you truly believe in your personal philosophy or religious faith—if you are committed, mind and soul, to your world view—you may well be capable of achieving remarkable feats of mind and body that [we] may only speculate about."

Bernie Siegel, M.D., a surgeon and professor at Yale University, describes some of the benefits of meditation: "It tends to lower or normalize blood pressure, pulse rate, and the levels of stress hormones in the blood. It produces changes in brain-wave patterns, showing less excitability. . . . Meditation also raises the pain threshold and reduces one's biological age. . . . In short, it reduces wear and tear on both body and mind, helping people live better and longer."

Many journalists, like Bill Moyers, have long noted the relation of mind and body to health. Here is what Moyers says in his introduction to the book *Healing and the Mind*, based on the Public Broadcasting System's television series.

> I suppose I've always been interested in the relation of mind
> and body, growing up as I did in a culture that separated them

distinctly. . . . Yet every day in this divided world of mind and body, our language betrayed the limitations of our categories. "Widow Brown must have died of a broken heart—she never got sick until after her husband was gone." My parents talked about our friend the grocer, who "worried himself sick," and my uncle Carl believed that laughter could ease what ailed you long before Norman Cousins published his story about how he coped with serious illness by watching Marx Brothers movies and videos of "Candid Camera."

In recent years, Western medical science has begun to take a closer look at mind and body, and to examine the connection between the mind, emotions, and health. In the 1970s researchers found evidence of what they called neurotransmitters, chemical messengers to and from the brain. Some neurotransmitters, called endorphins and enkephalins, act as natural painkillers. Others seem to be related to particular states of mind, such as anger, contentment, or mental illness.

Research is continuing on the biological links between the brain, the nervous system, and the immune system. Although Western medical science is not the topic of this book, discoveries in this area are very interesting. New evidence about mind and body is always welcomed and may benefit many people. However, the basic idea behind the research is actually very old. Buddhism has believed in the importance of the mind for many centuries, long before modern theories of molecular biology were advanced.

## TIBETAN MEDICINE'S APPROACH
## TO SPIRITUAL HEALING

In Buddhism, the mind generates healing energies, while the body, which is solid and stable, grounds, focuses, and strengthens them. The main text of Tibetan medicine is the *Four Tantras (Gyud zhi)*, which Tibetans see as a *terma*, or mystical revelation, discovered by Trawa Ngonshey in the eleventh century. According to these ancient texts, the root of all sickness of mind and body is grasping at "self." The poisons of the mind that arise from this grasping are ignorance, hatred, and desire.

Physical sicknesses are classified into three main divisions. Disharmony of wind or energy, which is generally centered in the lower body and is cold by nature, is caused by desire. Disharmony of bile, which is generally in the upper body and is hot, is caused by hatred. Disharmony of phlegm, which is generally centered in the head and is cold by nature, is caused by ignorance. These categories—desire, ignorance, and hatred—as well as the temperatures associated with them can still be very useful today in determining which meditation exercises might be most helpful, depending on the individual's emotional state and nature.

According to Tibetan medicine, living in peace, free from emotional afflictions, and loosening our grip on "self" is the ultimate medicine for both mental and physical health.

What is this "self" that has come up now several times in this book? The Buddhist view of self is sometimes difficult for people outside this tradition to understand. Although you can meditate without knowing what the self is, some background on the self will make it easier to do the healing exercises presented later.

Language can be tricky when we are talking about great truths. In an everyday sense, it is quite natural and fine to talk about "myself" and "yourself." I think we can agree that self-knowledge is good, and that selfishness can make us unhappy. But let's go a bit further and examine the deeper truth about self as Buddhists see it.

## WHY WE ARE SUFFERING

Our minds create the experience of both happiness and suffering, and the ability to find peace lies within us. In its true nature, the mind is peaceful and enlightened. Anyone who understands this is already on the path to wisdom.

Buddhism is centered on the principle of two truths, the absolute truth and the relative truth. The absolute is that the true nature of our minds and of the universe is enlightened, peaceful, and perfect. By the true nature of the mind, Nyingma Buddhism means the union of awareness and openness.

The relative or conventional truth is that in the whole spectrum of ordinary life—the passing, impermanent earthly life of birth and death that Buddhists call *samsara*—the world is experienced as a place of suffering, ceaseless change, and delusion, for the face of the true nature has been obscured by our mental habits and emotional afflictions, rooted in our grasping at "self."

In Western thought, "self" usually means personhood, or the ego consciousness of "I, me, and mine." Buddhism includes this meaning of self, but also understands "self" as any phenomenon or object—anything at all—that we might grasp at as if it were a truly existing entity. It could be the self of another person, the self of a table, the self of money, or the self of an idea.

If we grasp at these things, we are experiencing them in a dualistic way, as a subject grasping at an object. Then the mind begins to discriminate, to separate and label things, such as the idea that "I" like "this," or "I" don't like "this." We might think, "this" is nice, and attachment comes in, or "that" is not so nice, then pain may come. We may crave something we do not have, or fear losing what we have, or feel depressed at having lost it. As our mind gets tighter and tighter, we feel increasing excitement or pain, and this is the cycle of suffering.

With our "relative" or ordinary mind, we grasp at self as if it were firm and concrete. However, self is an illusion, because everything in the experience of samsara is transitory, changing, and dying. Our ordinary mind thinks of self as something that truly exists as an independent entity. But in the Buddhist view, self does not truly exist. It is not a fixed or solid thing, but a mere designation labeled by the mind. Neither is self an independent entity. In the Buddhist view, everything functions interdependently, so that there is nothing that has a truly independent quality or nature.

In Buddhism, the law of causation is called *karma*. Every action has a commensurate effect; everything is interdependent. Seeds grow into green shoots, then into trees, then into fruits and flowers, which produce seeds again. That is a very simple example of causation. Because of karma, our actions shape the world of our lives. Vasubandhu, the greatest Mahayana writer on metaphysics, said: "Due to karma [deeds] various worlds are born."

Grasping creates negative karma—our negative tendencies and habits. But not all karma is negative, although some people mistakenly think of it this way. We can also create positive karma, and that is what healing is about. The tight grip on self creates negative karma. Positive karma loosens that grip, and as we relax, we find our peaceful center and become happier and healthier.

## WE ARE ALL BUDDHA

Buddhists believe that all beings possess Buddha-nature. In our true nature we are all Buddhas. However, the face of our Buddha-nature is obscured by karma and its traces, which are rooted in grasping at self, just as the sun is covered by clouds.

All beings are the same and are one in being perfect in their true nature. We know that when our mind is natural, relaxed, and free from mental or emotional pressures and situations that upset us, we experience peace. This is evidence that the uncontaminated nature of the mind is peaceful and not painful. Although this wisdom, the true nature that dwells in us, has been covered by mental defilements, it remains perfect and clear. Nagarjuna, founder of the Middle Way school of Mahayana Buddhism, writes:

Water in the earth remains unstained.
Likewise, in the emotional afflictions,
Wisdom remains unstained.

Nagarjuna speaks of peace and freedom as our own "ulti-mate sphere," which is within us all the time if we only realize it:

In the womb of a pregnant woman,
Although there is a child, we cannot see it.
Likewise, we do not see our own "ultimate sphere,"
Which is covered by our emotional afflictions.

Peace is within us; we need not look elsewhere for it. By using what Buddhists call "skillful means," including meditation exercises, we can uncover this ultimate sanctuary. Nagarjuna de-scribes the ultimate sphere—the great openness, the union of mind and universe—this way:

As by churning the milk, its essence-butter appears
    immaculately,
By purifying mental afflictions, the "ultimate sphere"
    manifests immaculately.
As a lamp in a vase does not manifest,
The "ultimate sphere" enveloped in the vase of mental
    afflictions is not visible for us.
In whatever part of the vase you make a hole,
From that very part, light from the lamp will shine forth.
When the vase of mental afflictions is destroyed through vajra-
    like meditation,
The light shines unto the limits of space.

Shakyamuni, the historical Buddha, says in *Haivajra:*

Living beings are Buddha in their true nature,
But their nature is obscured by casual or sudden afflictions.
When the afflictions are cleansed, living beings themselves are
    the very Buddha.

Buddhahood, or enlightenment, is "no-self." It is total, ever-lasting, universal peace, openness, selflessness, oneness, and joy. For most people, the prospect of total realization of enlighten-ment is very foreign and difficult to understand. The purpose of this book is not to go beyond self, not to be fully enlightened, but only to relax our grip on self a little bit, and to be happier and healthier. Even so, it may be helpful to have an idea of what is meant by total openness and oneness.

The stories that we hear about "near-death experiences," of nearly dying but coming back from death, can provide us with insight. Many people who have survived the process of dying describe traveling through a tunnel and being met by a white light that touches them, giving them a feeling of great bliss and peace. Yet the light is not something separate from that experience. The light *is* peace. And they are the light. They do not experience the light in the usual dualistic way, as someone seeing light, as a subject and an object. Instead, the light, peace, and person are one.

In one near-death story, a man tells of reviewing everything that happened in his life, from birth until death—not just one event after another, but his entire life simultaneously. And he didn't just see with his eyes or hear with his ears, or even know with his mind; he had a vivid and pure awareness of seeing, knowing, and feeling without distinctions among them. In such a case, when limits and restrictions are gone, there is oneness. With oneness, there is no suffering or conflict, because conflict exists only where there is more than one.

For Buddhists, such experiences are especially interesting because they could be a glimpse of the "luminous *bardo* of ultimate nature"—a transitional period after death that, for people who have some realization of the truth, transcends the realm of ordinary space, time, and concepts. But such stories are not just about the experience of death; they also tell us about the enlightenment that is possible while we are alive.

The enlightened mind is really not so foreign. Openness is here within us, although we may not always recognize it. We can all experience it at some important juncture in our life, or even as a glimpse amid our everyday existence. We don't have to be near death. Although near-death stories can be inspiring and interesting, enlightenment isn't just one story or another. It is not "this" experience, or "that" way of looking or being. Total openness is free from the extremes of "existing" and "not existing";

nor is it *both* "existing" *and* "not existing"—or *neither* "existing" *nor* "not existing." In other words, total openness cannot be contained in concepts and descriptions.

## THE PATH OF HEALING

Enlightenment is oneness, beyond grasping at self, beyond duality, beyond happy or sad, beyond positive or negative karma. However, when we talk of healing, as in this book, it is not necessary to be too concerned with enlightenment. Realizing the true nature of our minds is the ultimate healing, but the ordinary mind also has healing powers. We can use our everyday, dualistic minds to help ourselves. Most of the exercises in this book take this everyday approach to becoming more relaxed and happy.

So our aim is simply to go from negative to positive, from sickness to healing. If we are already in a positive state for the time being, we can learn how to maintain and enjoy that. However much we loosen our grasping, that much better will we feel.

On a long journey, we may want to keep the ultimate destination in mind, but it is good to take one day at a time and rest along the way. If we want to relax our grip on self, we shouldn't try too hard. It is better to take a gentle approach. Whatever steps we take, even if they are small, the most important thing is to rejoice in those small steps; then they become powerful. Always we should appreciate what we are able to do, and not feel bad about what we haven't done.

To be a little more open, a little more positive, a little more relaxed. These are the goals of this book. If we are newcomers to meditation and spiritual training, it is important to be practical, to use our knowledge of ourselves to see the right path to take. When we keep an open attitude, suggestions about specific healing meditations can help us swiftly along the path. The best guide of all is the wisdom within us. We are not restricted to a few methods of meditation. Instead, all of life—thinking, feeling, everyday activities and experiences—can be a means of healing.

# 2

# THE HEALING POWER
# OF MIND ~

WHEN I WAS six or seven years old, I spent some time playing with friends on the vast grassy fields where nomadic Tibetans live. It was one of those beautiful sunny summer days on the northern Tibetan plateau. The land was covered with a single green carpet of grass as far as the eye could see. All over there were spectacular patterns of blindingly colorful flowers. The air was still, but birds were flying about and singing their sweet music. Butterflies were dancing up and down in the wind. Honey-bees were busy collecting nectar from the flowers. From the heavenly deep blue sky, here and there a few clouds were trying to shade Mother Earth's enchanting beauty. The touch of the air was so gentle and light that no other sensation can ever compare to it. The atmosphere was utterly clean and peaceful, with not a trace of pollution or disharmony. The only sound was the sweet, soothing music of nature. Events happened naturally, with no deadline to rush for. No clock ticked to restrict us; only the cycles of sun and moon gave rhythm and measure to our lives.

The whole atmosphere was totally free, wide open, and overwhelmingly peaceful. I had no thoughts of the frigid and ruthless winter that was waiting to pounce upon us. I rolled around in the ever-welcoming, tolerant lap of the mother soil and ran barefoot all over the field, enjoying the sensual kisses of the moist grass. My whole existence, both body and mind, was totally absorbed in one single experience—joy.

Suddenly, pain shot into my right foot and my whole body contracted in agony. Now all that I felt and saw was transformed into this single experience—pain. At first I had no idea what had happened. Then I heard a buzzing sound coming from my foot. A bumblebee was caught between my toes, but I could not open them to release it. As much as it stung me, that much more did my toes clench. As my toes became tighter, my tormenter stung again and again, and my pain increased. Finally one of my friends rushed over and forced my toes open to release the bee. Only then did the pain cease.

If only we could see this clearly how mental grasping causes our troubles! When we tighten our grip on self, our physical, mental, and spiritual pain only grows. In our confusion, we grasp ever tighter and tighter, setting in motion the cycle of suffering that characterizes the world of samsara. Even when we are enjoying ourselves, pain can come at any moment, and so we often cling tightly to what we have, for fear of the possibility of loss.

According to the Buddhist Mahayana philosophy, we wander this world aimlessly, blind to the inner power that can liberate us. Our minds fabricate desires and aversions, and like a drunken person we dance wildly to the tune set by ignorance, attachment, and hatred. Happiness is fleeting; dissatisfaction hounds us. It is all like a nightmare. As long as we are convinced the dream is real, we are its slaves.

To wake up, we must clear the clouds from the true nature of our minds. Many centuries ago, an Indian prince named Siddhartha Gautama gave up his claims to royalty and, after long and deep meditation, realized the truth about life as it really is. In doing so, he became known as the Buddha. In Sanskrit, the word *buddha* means "awake." We, too, can wake up. The healing process is an awakening to the power of our own minds.

## MIND IS THE MAIN FACTOR

Like a physician, we must diagnose the sickness, abandon the cause of the problem, and apply the medicine that leads to good health. Asanga, the founder of the Mind Only school of Buddhism, writes:

> As it is necessary to diagnose the sickness, to abandon its cause,
> Attain the happiness of good health, and apply medicine for it,
> The suffering should be recognized, the cause should be abandoned,
> The remedy for cessation should be applied, and cessation attained.

In Buddhism, the diagnosis and remedy are contained in the four noble truths: the truth that we suffer, the truth about why we suffer, the truth that we can end our suffering, and the truth about the path that leads to freedom. Following that path is a choice we can make. Even while struggling with everyday difficulties, we can improve our lives. Mind is the key. By properly guiding and training our minds, we can experience the power of healing. The *Dharmapada* says:

> Mind leads phenomena.
> Mind is the main factor and forerunner of all actions.
> If one speaks or acts with a cruel mind,
> Misery follows, as the cart follows the horse.
> Phenomena are led by the mind.
> Mind is the main factor and forerunner of all actions.
> If one speaks or acts with a pure mind,
> Happiness follows, as a shadow follows its source.

Happiness that is real and long-lasting comes not from material or external circumstances, but through contentment and strength of mind. Dodrupchen writes:

Learned people realize that all happiness and suffering depend upon the mind and therefore seek happiness from the mind itself. Because they understand that the causes of happiness are complete within us, they do not rely on external sources. If we have this realization, then whether we face problems caused by either beings or physical matter, they will not be able to hurt us. Furthermore, this same strength of mind shall also be with us to provide peace and happiness at the time of our death.

The true nature of our minds is peaceful. By learning how to let go of unnecessary worries and stresses, we give joy the chance to shine. It all depends on our minds. Buddhists believe it is possible to transform emotions, that joy is not only possible but our right. We do not need to be dominated by worry. Letting go is a commonsense approach, it is not some strange attitude limited to a particular religion or philosophy. As the New Jerusalem Bible (Eccles. 30:5) says:

> Do not abandon yourself to sorrow,
>     do not torment yourself with brooding.
> Gladness of heart is life to anyone,
>     joy is what gives length of days.
> Give your cares the slip, console your heart,
>     chase sorrow far away;
> for sorrow has been the ruin of many
>     and is no use to anybody.
> Jealousy and anger shorten your days,
>     and worry brings premature old age.
> A genial heart makes a good trencherman,
>     someone who enjoys a good meal.

## HOW TO LIVE IN THE WORLD

Some people think of Buddhism as a religion for people who want to reach a state of bliss and then disappear into some kind of nonexistence away from other people. This is not at all an accurate picture of Buddhism. Buddhists believe in participating fully in life. The path of healing does not exclude problems and difficulties; in fact, it embraces them as a means of realizing our true nature.

We can take a practical approach to problems that appear to be totally negative. If we are in a stressful situation, we should recognize and make peace with it, thinking, "It's bad, but it's OK." If we do not become hysterical over the situation, stringing together a chain of negative perceptions about it, its impact will wear out, for like everything in life, this situation is impermanent and will change sooner or later. Knowing this, we can calmly take the next step toward healing, with a confident feeling that external situations cannot overpower our inner wisdom.

In the Buddhist view, emotions ultimately are neither good nor bad. We should accept and welcome all our feelings. At the same time, we need not be ruled by wild or destructive emotions. If we are vulnerable to cravings, attachments, confusion, or hatred, it is better to think about "what is right for me to do" rather than "what I want to do." As we enter the path of healing, we should strengthen our intentions. We should let our minds guide our emotions.

If we rely on anything outside ourselves as the ultimate source of satisfaction, we will feel like we are riding on a roller coaster of gratification and dissatisfaction. Grasping leaves us at the mercy of the ever-turning wheel of samsara, the passing world of pain and pleasure. When we let go of self and find our true peaceful center, we see that it is not so necessary to cling to the concepts of good and bad, happy and sad, this and that, "me" and "them." Many religions and philosophies advise against identifying too strongly with the self. The famous Hindu scriptures called the Upanishads compare this identification with a trap: "In thinking 'This is I' and 'That is mine,' [one] binds with his self, as does a bird with a snare."

Taking care of our true needs and those of others is the way to find peace, and to do this we can and often should involve ourselves in the world. Struggle is not necessarily bad. We can learn to see the struggles of life as interesting challenges. However, we must recognize that in seeking any goal, worldly or spiritual, grasping will exhaust us and entrap us in selfishness. The skill of living in a balanced way becomes easier when we know what we really need to live.

## WHAT IS IMPORTANT FOR HUMAN LIFE?

Food, clothing, shelter, health, care, and education are necessary to sustain one's precious human life. As members of human society, we need to respect each other and respect the basic needs and institutions that benefit other people. Beyond that, nothing external is worth our time, peace, energy, and wisdom—the great gifts of our life. The other commodities of living are mostly tools to satisfy our craving mind, worship and polish our ego, and tighten our grasping. As we accumulate mundane pleasures, our craving to race after more is aggravated. The *Lalitavistara-sutra* advises:

> Your enjoyment of the pleasures of desire,
> Like drinking salt water, will never bring satisfaction.

Rich and poor alike suffer because of external worries related to desire. Even millionaires suffer from anger, despair, depression. They enjoy little true rest and peace, but only worry about losing what they have or getting what they do not have. They cannot enjoy who they are, but live only for what they are attracted to or enslaved by. It is not that making money in itself causes suffering, but handing over one's life to the tyranny of external possessions is the killer of joy and peace.

In a similar way, poor people become trapped by the struggle for survival. They don't even dare to enjoy what little they have for fear of incurring more pain. When Mother Teresa was awarded the Nobel Peace Prize, she told this story: One day the missionary sisters in Calcutta brought an orphan child into their care and gave him a piece of bread. The child ate half but wouldn't eat the rest. When asked why he wasn't eating, he said: "If I eat all the bread now, where will my next bread come from?" Only after being assured that he would get more was the child able to eat the other half of the bread.

Despite the progress and material development of modern civilization, many people are derailed from a meaningful life. Whether rich or poor or comfortably in between, we must be careful not to cherish material pleasures at the cost of our own true nature. If we spend our energies only thinking about mundane things and how to win more of them—better food, a bigger house, more money, fame, and recognition, whatever is outside ourselves—we lose what is most valuable.

We focus our attention on everything that is far from ourselves—the farther from our true selves, the more important we think it is. We value our possessions and bodies above our minds, our appearance above our health, our careers over our home life. We identify with the body and view our mind merely as the body's tool—"the fungus on the brain," as someone once jokingly described it—we cut ourselves off from the true source of happiness. We accumulate possessions for our homes but do not take care of our minds and bodies, although the most important conditions for a home life are a happy mind and healthy body.

When I was growing up in Tibet, an acquaintance of mine was chopping wood and cut through his new shoe with the ax. Fortunately, his foot wasn't injured, but shoe leather is valued in a poor country like Tibet. His unpretentious remark was, "If I didn't have those shoes on, it would have been my foot, and that would heal. Too bad! It is my new shoe instead, and it will never be healed!" This is a very funny way of looking at things. But it is not uncommon for people to put material objects first, then the body, and finally the mind, which is exactly the opposite of how it should be.

Although we may say, "I want to be peaceful and strong,"

we actually value—and are rewarded for—being aggressive in order to earn our material needs, rather than being balanced or peaceful in order to nourish our inner strength. We spend more time and energy on our career than on building a home life with the family, although we claim to be working in order to have a happy home.

We live like honeybees, who usually dedicate their entire lives to collecting honey but then, at the end, give it all up to someone else, who receives the fruit of their life-long labor. We place more value on the amount of money earned—and the inflated lifestyle it buys—than on the purpose of the work, failing to consider whether the work benefits ourselves and others. We put our precious lives at risk in order to make money, so that we end up drinking to alleviate the pressure of work or getting sick with ulcers. Money has become the master, meaning, and ultimate goal for so many people.

If we try to work on our minds to improve our attitudes and qualities, modern society labels us selfish, impractical, and lazy. Materially productive people are praised highly, but not seekers of the spiritual path. If we stay at home, caring for the center and sanctuary of life, people treat us as incapable, unprofessional, and unskilled. The home has been reduced to a motel, a place to break for the night.

We have to give up some things in order to get others. How can we think of losing our precious peaceful center and the joyous life that naturally radiates from it, in order to experience a life full of problems? It seems that now not only everyday people but even many spiritual masters feel forced to pursue modern materialistic culture. An old story conveys the irony of this situation:

Once upon a time in India, seers predicted that in seven days there would be heavy rain and that whoever drank the rainwater would become insane. When the rain came, the king had saved plenty of pure water for himself, so he avoided becoming insane. But the people soon ran out of pure water and all went mad. Soon they started accusing the king of being insane. Therefore, in order to understand his people and to feel the same way they did, the king drank the rainwater and became insane like his subjects.

I am not suggesting that we can or should ignore the system of modern life. We cannot survive without the satisfaction of basic needs, and it is important for us to be practical and respect popular views. But we should try to put everything into perspective. It is essential to understand who we are, where we stand, what is truly valuable, and how to live in the world.

If we are careless and let our grasping mind become rigid and tight, our negative habits will eat away at our sense of peace. The *Udanavarga* says:

> From iron appears rust, and
> Rust eats the iron.
> Likewise, the careless actions that we perform,
> Due to karma, lead us to hellish lives.

A simple incident that took place early in my refugee life made a strong impression on me. With some friends, I had arrived in Kalimpong, a nice town in the Himalayan hills of India. At the top of a hill, near a cemetery, we stopped to make tea, as we were tired and hungry and hadn't enough money to go to a restaurant.

I went to find some rocks and wood to use as a stove. When I reached the other side of the hill, I caught sight of an old monk with a big face and small, shining eyes, probably in his late seventies or early eighties. By his round face and high cheekbones I recognized him as a lama from Mongolia. He was sitting in a very small room in the back of an old house with his door and window wide open. The size of the room might have been eight feet by eight feet. In that same little room, he meditated, read, cooked, slept, and talked with people, sitting cross-legged on the same bed the whole day. He had a small altar with a few religious objects and scriptures on a little shelf on the wall. At his bedside was a very tiny dining table that was also his study desk. Near the table was a small charcoal stove on which he was cooking a little meal for himself.

His face broke into a kind and joyful smile as he asked me, "What are you looking for?" I said, "We just got here and I am looking for some fuel and materials for a stove to make tea." In a soothing voice he said, "There is not much to eat, but would you like to join me to share the meal I am preparing?" I thanked him, but declined. My friends were waiting. Then he said, "Then wait a minute. I will finish cooking and you can borrow my stove. There is still enough charcoal in it for you to make tea."

I was stunned by what I saw. He was very old, and it seemed as if he could be having a hard time taking care of himself. Nevertheless, his tiny eyes were full of kindness, his graceful and dignified features were full of joy, his open heart was full of eagerness to share, and his mind was peaceful. He was talking to me as an old friend although he had just seen me for the first time. A kind of tingling sensation of happiness, peace, joy, and amazement went through my body. I felt that because of his mental nature and spiritual strength he shone as one of the richest and happiest people in the world. Yet in terms of the materialistic world, he was homeless, jobless, hopeless. He had no savings, no income, no family support, no social benefits, no government support, no country, no future. Above all, as a person who was a refugee in a foreign country, he could hardly even communicate with the local people. Even today when I remember him, I can't help but shake my head in amazement and celebrate in my heart for what he was. I would like to add that he is not the only person of that nature I have seen. There are many simple but great beings.

## SETTING OUT ON THE HEALING PATH

Relaxing our hold on self brings us peace of mind, and with that nothing can harm us. Even if we suffer, the right attitude will help us carry our emotions more lightly. To benefit from meditation techniques aimed at strengthening our mind, right from the start it is important to hear what is taught without preconceptions and judgments. If we find something that is understandable and sensible for our needs, we should direct all our feeling and intention into putting the technique into practice, without hesitation, expectation, or doubt. Belief is a powerful healing agent. Simply by opening our minds, we may be surprised by our own inner strength.

Training the mind develops warmth of spirit and can guide us to an awareness that is more open and flexible. Although not every technique that I will introduce here is in the traditional form of training taught in the scriptures, all the suggestions are based on the principles and wisdom of Buddhism. The aim is to bring forth inner peace by developing such qualities as positive perception, the skill of turning everything that happens to us into a support instead of an obstacle.

Another important quality is devotion, which is necessary in any spiritual practice, but it does not need to be taken in a religious sense. For someone who prefers a secular approach, devotion could simply mean a cultivation of inner wisdom and a deep appreciation of ourselves, other people, and the world at large. Prayer is the way a spiritual person has of channeling energy into devotional expression rather than wasting it in aimless chatter. The secular version of prayer is to express our happy and joyous feelings in our own words, which we can say silently or even out loud.

For Mahayana Buddhists, who are interested in transforming problems and dissolving self, compassion is considered an especially healing tool. When we reach out to others, the rigidity of self begins to soften. Although the ultimate goal of spiritual training is to become free from relying on anything outside the mind, Buddhism recommends involvement in the world as a positive practice along the true path. This could include serving others, creating organizations and institutions to help others, providing protection, giving gifts, saying prayers, and paying respect. Even the small social encounters of life can have a powerful benefit when we learn to enjoy and respect whomever we are with. Shantideva writes:

When you speak, speak with ease, relevance, clarity, and
    pleasantness,
Without desire and hatred,
In gentle tones and at moderate length.
When you look, look with honest and loving eyes, thinking:
"By depending on this kind person
I will become fully enlightened."

By just allowing our minds to be caring, peaceful, and relaxed, our daily activities and work—even our breathing—can become part of our healing practice and we will gain strength spontaneously. If we are open to it, our ordinary life will turn into a life of healing. Then, even though we may not be spending hours in formal sitting meditation, our life will be meditation in action.

Most of the exercises in this book are aimed at transforming emotions by visualizing our problems and going from negative to positive. Another approach to meditation is to go beyond positive and negative, by opening ourselves to our feelings and experiencing our mind just "as it is." Actually, meditation aimed at transforming problems is most effective when it incorporates positive feelings and also openness. First we concentrate, and then we end the exercise by relaxing and being at one with whatever we are experiencing.

After we learn some of the traditional meditations and exercises, we can become skillful in applying our own remedies to everyday problems. The concept of "I" may be more flexible than we thought. We can experiment and learn to be more playful and less fixed in our perspective. For instance, when a problem appears to be serious, we can find relief by discovering some humor within it. Or if we are under pressure at work, we can feel more relaxed and spacious. Since words have great power, we could tell ourselves, "The pressure is on, but I feel completely relaxed." We can be aware of our breathing in a relaxed way, and notice and feel the space and the air around us, and in this way actually feel that we have less pressure and more space.

When emotions feel overwhelming, some people find it helpful to practice openness rather than trying to transform the problem. Merging with openness will be discussed in the next chapter, but it will not surprise anyone who has read this far that the principle behind this approach is to let go of "self."

If someone who can't swim falls into the ocean, that person will grasp at the water and sink like a rock. A good swimmer who has trained knows how to relax and become one with the vast ocean. Learning how to swim takes practice, and it helps to have some guidance as we begin. It is the same way with training our minds, which is what the rest of this book is about.

# 3

# GETTING STARTED ⁓

OVER THE CENTURIES, Buddhism has developed a vast reservoir of knowledge about the mind. Especially as we begin to learn meditation, all the suggestions and ideas may feel overwhelming. It's best to keep our practice simple. Set attainable goals and strive for them with positive energy. Don't worry about difficulties, but instead feel glad about any benefits that come. Even negative experiences or so-called shortcomings can be a benefit if we view them positively.

When meditating, we should relax and let go, rather than chasing our worries and desires. We usually sit down to meditate, but much of what we learn about meditation can be carried into all our daily activities. Words are necessary to describe how to meditate and how to bring the right attitude to our lives. However, the important thing is to practice and feel, without being overly concerned about concepts, categories, or rules. Be patient and open, and work with what your own life brings to you.

## CHOOSING A PLACE

The best place to practice spiritual training in healing is a peaceful, pleasant place where there are few distractions, where the mind can be calm and the body comfortable, and where we can feel alert, spacious, and happy.

Sages of the past have praised a variety of places, depending on the character of the practitioner, the practice, and the season. Among the favored solitary locations are those that have a clear, far-reaching view, like the top of a sky-kissing mountain or the lap of a prosperous field. Some practitioners have found solace in the forest, among the trees and wild animals and birds singing their ageless song of joy and playing free from fear. Others suggest training by the ocean with its dancing, ever-changing waves or a river with its mighty, natural flow. Still others have trained in the dry caves of empty valleys where there is an atmosphere of sublime peace.

If we do not live in such natural settings, we should find a pleasant place in our own home space, make the best of it, and rejoice.

Choose the quietest room or corner of a room of your home, during a time when there will be few disturbances from the telephone, children, roommates, spouse, or friends. Then feel good: good about the place, the time, and the opportunity to have this place and time. Arouse joy at this chance to realize the spiritual meaning of your life.

Generally, it is better for beginners to practice alone, in a place that presents no obstructions. After gaining strength in the training, we can seek harder situations that require more tolerance and discipline—with obstacles such as disturbances from people or noise from traffic—to strengthen ourselves in using the hardships that come our way. Finally, when we are ready, we can practice dwelling in the worst situations, with all kinds of mental temptation and emotional turmoil. By practicing diligently in this way, eventually we will be able to face and transform any situation into a source of strength without losing our peaceful mind. Wherever we live will then become a palace of enlightenment and purity. Every event will be a teaching. After that the place won't matter; the only need will be to choose a place where we can best serve others.

## CHOOSING A TIME

Although any time is fine for training, peace and calm are helpful for a beginner. Early morning is good, for then the day itself is fresh and the mind is clear. However, some might feel relaxed and ready to meditate in the evening. Choose a time, observe it regularly, and be happy with it. If you can, allow nothing to interfere with your regular practice.

Whatever meditation or healing exercise we do, we should give ourselves to it. We should not dream about the future or make plans in our heads. Do not run after the past or grasp at the present. All kinds of thoughts or mental experiences may arise during meditation, but instead of grasping at them, let them come and go.

Practice every day. Even if we meditate for a short time, the consistency will keep the contemplative experience alive and steady us on the path of healing.

How long should we meditate? Your mind is the healer, so the answer depends on your needs and abilities. You could meditate for a few minutes, for twenty minutes, or for an hour. You could meditate for many hours, with rest periods, over a long period of time. Don't be overly concerned with time, but rather consider what feels right.

It's especially good to practice when we are happy, healthy, and relatively free of problems. Then, when we face suffering—which will certainly come—we will have the skillful means ready to apply. Unfortunately, it takes the experience of suffering for many of us to turn our minds toward spiritual solutions. When we are in the midst of pain and confusion, we may have less clarity, energy, and opportunity for training. Dodrupchen advises:

> It's very difficult to practice healing when we actually come face to face with difficult situations. Thus, it's important to

experience spiritual exercises, so that when unfavorable circumstances arise we are ready. It makes a great difference if we use a training in which we are experienced.

## POSTURE

The essential goal of any of the various postures for meditating is to relax the muscles and open the channels in the body so that energy and breath can flow naturally through them. Whatever posture makes our body straight and relaxed, but not stiff, will produce a natural flow of energy and allow the mind to be calm and flexible. The purpose of the physical postures is summarized in this popular Tibetan saying:

> If your body is straight, your channels will be straight.
> If your channels are straight, your mind will be straight.

One of the most popular Buddhist meditation positions is called the lotus posture, in which one sits cross-legged on the floor with the right foot on the left thigh and the left foot on the right thigh. Most Westerners find the half-lotus easier, with one ankle resting on the fold of the opposite leg. If you sit on a small cushion, your torso will be raised up a bit in a way that you may find is open and relaxed.

Your hands are placed on your lap, right hand over left with tips of thumbs touching, and palms up. The elbows should be slightly away from the body, in a natural, winglike position, instead of being cramped or pressed inward. The chin is lowered to allow the neck to bend slightly, so that it feels natural to focus the eyes a yard or two in front, at the level of the tip of the nose. The tip of the tongue is gently touching the upper palate. The most important element of all is to keep the spine straight.

Some people may find this posture very difficult if they have back problems. You may want to sit on a chair to meditate, but make sure the chair allows you to keep your spine straight rather than slumping. Whatever posture you choose, remember that the purpose is not to be uncomfortable. The Buddha himself, after years of experimenting with ascetic practices, gave up mortification of the body. You should be comfortable enough so that your mind can relax and concentrate.

It's best to meditate in a sitting posture, but really our mind is capable of healing wherever we are and under any circumstance, as long as we are aware.

## RELAXATION

To release the struggles of our mind—the conceptual and emotional pressures that grip us—we should relax the tightness of our muscles when we meditate. If tension is gathered anywhere in your muscles, bring awareness to that area and release the tightness. Relaxation provides a calm atmosphere in which we can light the candle of healing energy. However, relaxation does not mean indulging in a lazy, careless, semiconscious, or sleepy state of mind. At times we may need to rest and be sleepy, but the most effective meditation is awake, alert, and clear. This is the way to touch our peaceful, joyous nature.

Allow yourself to stay relaxed in the transition from meditation back to your daily routine. Get up slowly and ease your mind into your activities. This way, you bring a spacious mind into your life.

## CREATING MENTAL SPACE

Few of us give ourselves completely to what we are doing. We bring our job problems home and so have no chance to enjoy our home life. Then we take our home problems to work and cannot devote ourselves to our job. While trying to meditate, we fondle our mental images and feelings, which gives us no real chance to concentrate. We end up having no life to live, as we are always dwelling in the past or future.

If we cluttered up our homes with too much furniture, we would have no place to live. If our minds are cluttered with plans, concerns, thoughts, and emotional patterns, we have no space for our true selves.

Many people feel their lives are too crowded to meditate. Even when they have time at home to meditate, they feel too distracted. To bring our full attention and energy to our home lives, and to meditation, we need mental space.

We can consciously create space for ourselves. We can decide to leave our worries about work behind us. If it is helpful, we could visualize these worries in the form of papers and computers that are safely back in the office. We could even imagine borderlines separating our work lives from home. Or we could create a protective tent of energy or light in our minds, enclosing us in our home and granting complete privacy for what we are doing now.

Meditation can be a haven of warmth and space, but we may feel resistance to meditating or think of it as a chore. One way to create an open and relaxed feeling is to go back to the atmosphere of childhood.

Since childhood, we have learned and experienced a lot of wonderful things in this generous world. However, it is easy to be caught up in today's frantic lifestyle. We can become like silkworms trapped by their own silk. We reach a stage where we suffocate ourselves with our own views, feelings, habits, and reactions.

Thinking back, we remember that as children a day seemed to last for a long time, more like the way we experience a month now. A year was so long there was no end to it. Gradually our perception changed. Our preoccupations, concepts, and attachments grew day by day. Now the open space is no longer there in our minds. As we grew, we felt time become shorter and shorter, and now a year passes in the blink of an eye. It is not because time actually became shorter, but because we do not have the mental space to feel open and free. We run around at full speed, and crowd our minds with a houseful of thoughts, concepts, and emotions. When our minds are calm, we feel every minute of time, but if our minds chase after everything going on around us, we feel that the day has ended before it has even begun.

Touching childhood memories can help us open up. As a meditation, go back to a positive memory from when you were young and had few worries, passions, or pressures. The exact memory isn't as important as the feeling of space and freedom. Rather than standing outside the memory and thinking about it, allow the feeling to expand and go within it. Experience the feeling and remain in it, without other thoughts. Let yourself feel and be one with yourself as a child. The past and present, the child and "me," all are one in spacious union. Contemplate and rest within this open feeling again and again. Finally, bring that feeling to the present moment of your life.

If bad experiences in your childhood come up instead of peaceful and spacious feelings, then you can use the approach outlined later in the healing exercises to purify, nourish, and heal the injured image and visualize that your inner child has become happy, healthy, and cheerful.

We can contact this spacious feeling anytime: for example, if we are having difficulty sitting down to meditate, or whenever we want to bring a sense of freedom and enjoyment to our lives. To reach the child within us, we can also enjoy childhood activities—games like yo-yo, juggling, and jump rope—or appreciate trees, flowers, water, and the beauty of nature. We can look at the night sky and stars through the eyes of wonder that we had as a child, and enjoy being out in the night air as we did then. These feelings can be ours now as adults when we bring them to the present moment. Doing so will help us forget our worries for a while and submerge us in the womb of childhood once again.

Spending time in solitude with nature, especially watching

the infinite space of the sky from a mountaintop, will help us make our minds spacious. But the most effective way to open up a peaceful space in our minds is meditation. Instead of crowding our minds with negative views and feelings, if we can get back to the skylike nature of mind, a dawn of peace and wisdom can then arise.

## BREATHING

In any kind of meditation, it is important to breathe naturally and calmly. Contemplation of our breathing, the mind's awareness of the breath, in and out, is in itself a foundation for realizing our true nature. Highly experienced meditators use this approach as a means to realize selflessness. Although in our healing exercises we will not be concerned with going beyond concepts of self, awareness of breathing can be very useful for other purposes. For example, it is a good way to calm ourselves, focus our minds, and establish a flow of energy that enables healing to progress.

At the beginning, you may feel it is impossible to concentrate fully on the simple act of breathing in and out. It can be shocking to see how fast the mind moves. Do not worry about the coming and going of thoughts or images. Gently bring your consciousness back to your breathing, and give your awareness completely to this. By just allowing our minds to touch and unite with the natural process of breathing, we can release stress and feel more relaxed.

Because of its importance in the higher practice of meditation, contemplation of breathing will be discussed in more detail in chapter 12. For now, consider using the contemplation of breathing as a preliminary to any healing exercise. Awareness of breathing is also a very powerful method to release any difficult emotion that has us in a viselike grip. As we'll see in the healing exercises, a particularly helpful technique is to concentrate on your relaxed exhalations. In this way, grasping is relaxed.

## VISUALIZATION

One of the best tools in healing is visualization, which can transform our mental patterns from negative to positive. Some beginners at meditation regard visualization as a difficult or unusual mental activity. Actually, it is quite natural, for we think in images all the time. When we think of our friends or family, or imagine ourselves at a lovely beach or mountain lake, we see these images in our minds quite vividly. In meditation we visualize for a particular purpose, but the mental process is the same. With practice, we can get better at it.

Although visualization has a long heritage in Tibetan Buddhist practice, people who have no knowledge of or interest in Buddhism have found the technique extremely helpful. For instance, some professional athletes visualize to improve their performance and realize their full potential.

Positive images inspire all sorts of people in all kinds of activities. I know of a music teacher in Boston who overcame stage fright using her own improvised approach. Although she's a trained singer with a splendid voice, she dreaded her weekly duties as the cantor at a local synagogue. One Sabbath before the service, she wept so violently that she suddenly realized how crippling her fears had become. That's when she made up her mind to enjoy herself instead! To help herself do this, she sat somewhere quiet and imagined herself leading the prayer successfully, singing in a way that felt good to her but without being overly worried about the melodies that had been difficult in practice.

She imagined what it would be like to be very confident about her singing. In her mind, she heard the beautiful sound of her own voice, giving delight to the congregation. She envisioned the whole scene of the prayer service and felt a lovely, expansive sense of gladness and inspiration at being able to share the music with everyone.

She now is happy in her singing, and is not bothered if she

feels a bit nervous ahead of time. In the classes she teaches, she suggests to her music students that they also use their imagination to learn how to be more relaxed and bring joy to their singing.

In meditation, it's best to keep your eyes open or partly open, in order to stay wakeful and in this world. However, it may be helpful for some beginners to close their eyes at first. The most important point in visualizing is to call up the positive image with warmth and whole-heartedness. Give your full attention to the mental object, become totally absorbed in it. Allow the mind and the object to become one. If we see the image in our minds half-heartedly or in a distracted way, our concentration is limited. Then it is as if we were staring blankly at an object just with our eyes, instead of with our whole being. Tsongkhapa, the founder of the Gelug school of Tibetan Buddhism, wrote: "Master Yeshe De has rightly negated the way that some people meditate in blankness by staring with their eyes at the image before them. 'Abiding in contemplation' has to develop in the mind, not in the senses such as the eyes."

For beginners especially, the key is to feel the presence of what you are imagining. Your visualization doesn't need to be elaborate or detailed; the clarity and stability of your mental images are what matters.

## CONCENTRATION

For any spiritual training or mental activity, we need concentration. Learning how to concentrate makes our minds strong, clear, and calm. Concentration protects our inner wisdom, like a candle flame sheltered from the wind.

For Buddhists, concentration on an object with spiritual significance will generate positive energy, blessings, and virtuous karma. However, we can train our minds to concentrate by practicing on virtually anything, whether it is a physical object or a mental image, regardless of whether it is spiritually meaningful.

Buddhist training to strengthen concentration involves two methods: inward and outward. The inward method is to concentrate on your own body, for example by seeing the body in the form of a deity or as a body of bones. We can also concentrate on elements of the body such as the breath, or the body as seen in the pure form of light or joy. The outward method is to concentrate on images, Buddha "pure lands," or other visualizations.

If we are unable to concentrate our minds, even years of practice will yield little insight, despite the merits of the effort. Shantideva reminds us:

> The Buddha who has realized the truth has said:
> All the recitations and ascetic trainings
> You have practiced even for a long time,
> If you have done them with a wandering mind,
> Will bear little fruit.

The first step in developing concentration is to bring our restless mind down to earth. In the healing exercises presented later, we'll see some techniques for focusing the scattered mind that can improve our ability to meditate as well as our emotional outlook.

Once we feel grounded mentally, we can deepen our ability to concentrate. Experienced meditators sometimes practice honing their concentration by visualizing a long, narrow pipe and using their imagination to look through it. Another mental exercise involves concentrating on a single tiny spot instead of a larger image.

If we need to work on concentration, awaken our minds, or sharpen our senses, we should focus for a while on developing mental discipline. However, often our minds are too discriminative and sensitive. If your mind feels trapped or suppressed, it's best not to force it rigidly into concentration. Those who feel burdened by mental stress and worries can find it very soothing to open up their awareness instead of focusing in a concentrated manner.

## OPENING

One way to break through the feeling of emotional suffocation is to go someplace high where you can have a far-reaching view, such as the top of a mountain or a building. If the sky is very clear, sit with your back to the sun. Concentrate on the depth of the open sky without moving your eyes. Slowly exhale and experience the openness, vastness, and voidness.

Feel that the whole universe has become one in the vast openness. Think that all phenomena—trees, mountains, and rivers—have dissolved spontaneously into the open sky. Your mind and body have dissolved there too. All have vanished like clouds disappearing from the sky. Relax in the feeling of openness, free from boundaries and limitations. This exercise is not only effective for calming the mind but can also generate higher realization.

If you cannot go to such a place, choose any spot from which you have a good view of the sky or from which you can at least visualize the open sky.

## MERGING IN ONENESS

Merging with oneness means being one with whatever we are experiencing. It sometimes helps in the beginning to describe oneness in words: for example, that it is like being a swimmer at one with the vast ocean. But actually words are not necessary for the experience of oneness and openness. We simply let go of our struggles and relax the need to put labels such as "good" or "bad" on experiences. We drop expectations about how we should feel or want to feel, and instead allow ourselves to be with the feeling or to go within it. By merging with experiences or feelings, the character of experience can change. By allowing ourselves to be just as we are in the present moment, the walls of our discriminations and sensitivities will soften, or fall away altogether. Our minds and hearts open, and our energy flows. This is a powerful healing.

# MINDFULNESS

Learning to live in the moment is a great and powerful skill that will help us in everything we do. To "be here now," relaxed and engaged in whatever we are doing, is to be alive and healthy. In Buddhism, the awareness of what is happening right now is called mindfulness.

In everyday life, mindfulness is an alert mind that is aware of every aspect that is going on, and what to do, without being scattered. In meditation, mindfulness is giving ourselves completely to our breathing, or whatever the exercise is.

Mindfulness is giving full attention to the present, without worries about the past or future. So often, we borrow trouble from the future by constantly thinking about what might befall us tomorrow, instead of dealing with one day at a time.

In Buddhism, the emphasis is on this very moment. We can guide our minds to live in the present. To do this, we need to firmly establish a habit of total attention to what we are doing now. For every undertaking, we should consciously decide to keep other ideas, feelings, and activities out and give ourselves to what we are doing.

To be mindful doesn't mean to become emotionally intense or to stir up hosts of concepts in order to watch what we are thinking or doing. On the contrary, the mind is relaxed and calm, and therefore sharply aware of every event as it is, without conceptual and emotional struggle. However, when we notice that our mind is wandering, we should gently but firmly bring ourselves back to the present and to what we are doing. For most of us, especially in the beginning, we may need to do this again and again. As Shantideva says:

> Again and again, examine
> Every aspect of your mental and physical activities.
> In brief, that is the very way of observing mindfulness.

Even if we are instructed in meditation or spiritual training, we need mindfulness and awareness, otherwise the mind will run about like a wild beast, unable to remain focused or at rest even for a few moments. Then what will we gain from our mere physical participation in meditation? Mindfulness is so vital that Shantideva pleads:

> I beg with folded hands
> Those who wish to guard their minds:
> "Please preserve mindfulness and awareness
> Even at the cost of your own life."

The fruit of mindfulness is the protection it provides in all kinds of turmoil and difficulty. According to Shantideva:

> So, I shall hold and guard
> My mind properly.
> Without the discipline of guarding my mind,
> What is the use of other disciplines?
> If I were in the midst of an uncontrolled wild crowd,
> I would be alert and careful of hurting my wounds.
> Likewise, while I live among undisciplined people
> I should guard my mind against hurting its wounds.

With mindfulness and awareness, we learn to be patient or to act, as the occasion calls for. Patience then becomes a transforming energy. Shantideva says:

> When you want to move or want to talk,
> First examine your mind,
> And then, with firmness, act in the proper way.
> When you feel desire or hatred in your mind,
> Do not act or speak, but remain like a log.

The practice of mindfulness should not result in stress. If it does, it may be a sign that we are trying too hard—that we are grasping at "mindfulness" itself, that we need to relax a little and be less self-conscious. Ven. W. Rahula writes:

Mindfulness, or awareness, does not mean that you should think and be conscious, "I am doing this" or "I am doing that." No. Just the contrary. The moment you think, "I am doing this," you become self-conscious, and then you do not live in the action, but you live in the idea "I am," and consequently your work too is spoilt. You should forget yourself completely, and lose yourself in what you do.

By remaining in a relaxed and spacious mood, we can live in a spontaneous stream of mindfulness and awareness. Our minds will become steadier, instead of constantly fragmenting into scattered thoughts and wildly chasing the past or future. After a while, our concentration will improve and we will find it easier to meditate. Learning how to enjoy and be in the present moment leads to openness and timeless time. By being mindful, we find the peace within ourselves.

## ENLIGHTENED ATTITUDE

In Mahayana Buddhism, spiritual practice is perfected through compassion. We should develop the attitude that "I am doing this spiritual training for the service, happiness, benefit, and enlightenment of all beings," or, "I am training in order to make myself a proper tool to serve and fulfill the needs of all beings." In the scriptures this is called the enlightened attitude.

This intention to dedicate our training to others is a powerful way to open our closed, restricted hearts. It produces a strong spiritual energy—a blessing—and sows in us the seed of enlightenment. If we develop and maintain this "enlightenment mind," then whatever we do will spontaneously become a spiritual training and means of benefit for all. Even for someone who is not religious, it will be very helpful to reflect upon his or her link to family, friends, community, and all people everywhere, instead of pursuing training merely for selfish goals.

Opening to compassion can be difficult, and we can be sub-

other disciple, in the presence of the Buddha himself, about how any situation can inspire the power of healing in our minds. Here is what Manjushri says in the *Avatamsaka-sutra*:

> When a bodhisattva sees people who have lots of love, he should think: "May all beings have lots of love and devotion to the Dharma." When the bodhisattva sees people with lots of dislike, he should think: "May all beings have the feeling of dislike toward all conditioned phenomena so they will strive for liberation." When a bodhisattva sees beings with happiness, he should think: "May all beings be extremely happy by obtaining the wealth of great joy of Buddhahood." When a bodhisattva sees beings with suffering, he should think: "May the sufferings of all beings be pacified by planting the root of wisdom in them."

## CONSISTENCE AND ENDEAVOR

We rush to find solutions while we are facing problems. But the moment those problems have eased, we neglect the discipline needed to strengthen and preserve our healing energies. When our problems resurface, we blame the practice, saying, "I did this training for so many years, but still have the same problems." The fault lies not with the training, but with the person who has moved away from the healing disciplines and their benefits.

Once you have trained a puppy not to jump up on the table, you should be consistent in never allowing it on the table. Otherwise, it will be confused and its habit of discipline will be forgotten. So we should maintain whatever positive habits we have achieved in any discipline, just as every month we pay insurance premiums to ensure security for sickness and old age.

Healing will come only by exerting ourselves and dedicating our life energy consistently to the practice. Even if we practice in seclusion for years, if we break the continuity of training for a few months, we could slip back and find ourselves at the beginning.

Once we have achieved a real breakthrough, if we continue

to practice consistently—even for as little as a few minutes daily—our steadiness of mind will not disappear but will continuously strengthen.

Even if we are not bright students or wise meditators, if we practice consistently, we can progress faster than those who claim to be scholars and propagators of wisdom. Quoting Jigme Lingpa, the founder of the Longchen Nyingthig tradition of Tibetan Buddhism, Paltrül Rinpoche writes:

> For a person who does not have diligence,
> Neither intelligence, power, wealth, nor strength will help him.
> He is like a captain with a boat but no sail.

A Tibetan proverb says:

> Scholars end up with empty hands in their armpits,
> While dedicated people smash even challenges like Mount Sumeru into dust.

If we are diligent, even if we are simple-minded, we can reach our goal. It is like the story of Lamchungpa, who became one of the famous ancient Buddhist sages known as the Sixteen Arhats. Simply by cleaning the sandals of other monks, he was able to understand the teachings of "the Bliss-gone," or Buddha. The First Dalai Lama retells the story:

> Lamchungpa's mind was very dull. Many disciples of the Buddha gave up trying to teach him. Then the Buddha instructed him to clean the sandals of the monks and to repeat two phrases, "Dust is cleaned. Defilements are cleaned," which he memorized with very great difficulty. After working with these for a long time, one day a thought came into his mind: "Oh, what did the Buddha mean by the 'cleaning of the dust' and the 'cleaning of defilements'? Is it the dust and defilements of the inside [mind] or of the external things [sandals]?" At that moment three new verses came into his mind:

This is not the dust of earth, but of desire.
Dust is the name of desire and not of the dust of earth.
Learned ones who have cleansed the dust
Attain awareness in the doctrine of the Bliss-gone.

This is not the dust of earth, but of hatred.
Dust is the name of hatred and not of the dust of earth.
Learned ones who have cleansed the dust
Attain awareness in the doctrine of the Bliss-gone.

This is not the dust of earth, but of ignorance.
Dust is the name of ignorance and not of the dust of
    earth.
Learned ones who have cleansed the dust
Attain awareness in the doctrine of the Bliss-gone.

Then he diligently contemplated the meaning of those lines and before long attained Arhathood, the state of total elimination of emotional and mental afflictions.

## BALANCE

Balance is essential to both meditation and daily living. Being too forceful and pushy only creates rigidity, stress, paranoia, and pain. Being too slack or lazy results in daydreams, delusions, and lack of focus and strength. To learn how to meditate, Paltrül Rinpoche advises us to pay heed to the story contained in the sutras:

Ananda, the main disciple of the Buddha, taught Shravana how to meditate. However, Shravana was not able to have good meditation because sometimes his mind was too tight and at other times too relaxed. When this case was presented to the Buddha, he asked Shravana: "Sir, when you were living at home, were you skilled in playing the guitar?"
He said, "Yes, very much so."
The Buddha asked, "Does the sound of the guitar come from tight strings or loose strings?"
He answered, "Neither, sir. It is produced by balanced strings."

Then the Buddha said, "That is what your mind needs, too."

Then, by meditating in a balanced manner, Shravana reached the fruition of his training.

In meditation, we give our full attention and energy to meditation, and in a way this takes effort. But we shouldn't feel strain, and in this way meditation is effortless. Like the guitar strings, we are tight but relaxed—in other words, alert but not straining. If we are lazy, our minds do not become steady and calm. If we strain, we burn up energy and end up grasping. Quoting Machig Labdron, the most famous female master of Tibet, Paltrül Rinpoche writes:

> The crucial point of meditative view lies
> In being tight and relaxed.

Flexibility is the key to maintaining the balance of our minds in everyday situations. Atisha, one of the greatest Indian Buddhist masters of the tenth century, wrote:

> Whenever your mind is too high,
> It is necessary to crush your pride
> By remembering the instructions of the teacher.
> Whenever your mind is too low,
> It needs to have inspiration.
> Whenever you face objects of desire or hatred,
> See them as illusions and apparitions.
> Whenever you hear unattractive things,
> See them as echoes.
> Whenever hurt comes to your body,
> Accept it as the result of your karma.

Like a figure skater who is balanced even while spinning and doing amazing feats on ice, we need to be aware of our center. If we go to extremes, we lose our peaceful center and become off-balance. For instance, in our relationships with other people, we need friendship and support, and we also need to be independent.

People fall into extremes in how they relate to others. Some parents suffocate their children in relationships of mutual overdependency. Other parents may fear emotional closeness and fail to give their children enough support. Yes, every person should be able to stand on his or her own two feet. But generally, intimacy is nourishing and allows children—and parents—to grow emotionally. Parents should talk to their children, involve themselves in their games and lives, and express their warm feelings of love. They should also allow them to grow as independent people. This is the balance we need.

Many grown children blame their parents for emotional problems, or rebel against anyone in authority. We may need to understand our past, but blame does not bring freedom. If we get stuck in resentment and anger, we can build toxins inside ourselves and cling to them in a way that harms us. Healing is the answer. See the past for what it is, then forgive and let go. This is the way to find peace.

Extreme self-reliance, the fear of relying on others, can stunt our emotional and spiritual growth. Some people reject the idea of relying on anyone except themselves. But by being too proud or too fearful, they deny themselves the benefit of their own spiritual training. They doubt that a teacher or specific teachings can help them, and their doubts keep them from healing. Total freedom from dependency on others is possible, but for most of us the attempt to be perfectly independent as we learn how to deal with problems is a mistake.

We need others to help make life less of a struggle. Support from family, friends, and community is very positive. At the same time, in our efforts to grow emotionally and spiritually, we should proceed at our own pace and abilities, not according to someone else's timetable. In every circumstance, we can eventually find balance if we are calm and relaxed.

## FEELING

When we are told an inspiring story, it is not hearing it, but *feeling* it that brings inspiration. The effective way of connecting with any source of healing is not just to *see* or perceive something as an object for healing, but to *feel* it with our whole being.

The way to practice the healing exercises is to center yourself in your heart  in your positive feelings. Do not just think, but feel also. It is true that the highest stage of spiritual attainment is beyond qualified, dualistic perceptions and feelings—beyond subject and object, beyond positive and negative, beyond an "I" who visualizes an image. However, for people like us who are struggling with pain and excitement, the immediate, appropriate goal is to try to turn negative views into positive ones, to heal our feelings of suffering, and to feel soothing joy from the depths of our hearts.

## SEEING OR FEELING WITH YOUR WHOLE BODY AND MIND

As we train, especially in the beginning, we will naturally localize our energies by looking at a visualized image with our eyes, or thinking about an object with our heads, or feeling something with our hearts.

For some practices, this approach is helpful. However, it can sometimes cause difficulty if it is practiced with too much intensity or strain in a way that localizes energy in only one part of the body.

For example, we may concentrate too much energy in our eyes when visualizing, or we may focus feeling too intensely in the area of the heart. In Tibet, this is explained in terms of "air," or energy, that flows to whatever part of the body the mind concentrates on. Too much energy in one area can cause strain, and even sickness.

The solution is simply to relax and give full attention to our concentration with our entire being, without struggle. In this way, we are seeing and feeling with our whole body, and the energy is magnified rather than being tightly localized. In everyday life, if you stare too hard at a computer screen, you may get headaches, unless you look in a more relaxed way. Similarly, singers can strain their vocal cords, unless they learn to relax and bring the sound up from the area of the abdomen with their breathing. If meditation is a strain, it is a sign to ease up and allow the mind and body to meditate in a relaxed way within the moment.

## THE POWER OF SECRECY

Often spiritual training becomes more effective when given as a secret instruction, kept as a secret treasure, and practiced in secret without confiding in anybody but the teacher. The ultimate goal of the teaching is to open us up, not to limit or isolate ourselves in seclusion. But especially at the beginning, we need to gather our energy and concentration. Secrecy can help us to do this.

If we use what we learn for dinner-table chatter or as a business commodity, a tool for mundane goals, we risk dispersing our energy and inspiration. When we keep the training secret, concentrated energy develops more effectively, just as an engine harnesses power to lift a rocket out of the earth's gravity field because the burning fuel is kept under great pressure rather than escaping randomly.

## KNOWING OUR STRENGTHS AND WEAKNESSES

We are all different, with individual temperaments and particular qualities of mind, but we can all find peace. As Shantideva says:

> Witnessing their own blood, some become braver and
> stronger.

Some, even when they see others' blood,
Faint and fall unconscious.
These reactions are due to the strength
Or cowardice of the mind.
So by disregarding the problems
Let your mind become invincible to sufferings.

All of us are perfect in our true nature, and this is our great strength. After understanding this, we should build on our individual strengths and heal our weaknesses.

Recognizing our weaknesses is sometimes difficult. Some of us are stone-hearted and arrogant. Some are angry and negative about everything. Some are drunk with money and power and indulge in constant self-gratification and wild ideas. If any of these afflictions describe us, we need to soften our rough, hard selves and find balance. Meditations on the sorrows, losses, and problems of this world can open our minds.

Unfortunately, if we are proud and willful, we are our own worst enemy, for it will be hard for us even to see our problems. So recognition of our faults is the important first step.

Then there are those of us who are depressed, weak, confused, or even suicidal. If we have no confidence in anything, it is better to contemplate inspiring trainings such as devotion, positive attitude, pure perception, compassion, and love. We should let go of worries and doubts, and believe in ourselves and the power of teachings.

To know ourselves, it can be very helpful to get advice from a teacher or skilled counselor. We do not need to go it alone; we can accept the gift of nurturance from friends and other people. At the same time, it is true that ultimately healing lies within us. In our truest selves, we can find the answers we need. The teachings of the ages provide the signposts. We need to bring warmth and creativity to the way we follow them.

# 5

# HOW TO DEAL WITH PROBLEMS ~

WE'VE ALREADY SEEN how problems are created by grasping at self, and that we can ease them by developing attitudes and skills to loosen this grasping. Now let's focus even more closely on some practical techniques in dealing with problems.

## AVOIDANCE

Usually we face problems in order to heal them, but not always. Sometimes the best approach is avoidance. For example, if your problem is mild or temporary—not a deep-rooted habit or a feeling of severe pain—ignoring it will be the sufficient and proper solution. It is not necessary or worthwhile to devote a lot of energy to such problems. If we don't mind them, these problems will go away.

At other times, we might have to avoid problems if we are not ready to face them, like a soldier who must temporarily retreat or rest before battle. If your problem is too strong, sharp, and fresh in your mind, you may not have the strength to face it or to apply any training directly to pacify it. Facing it too soon might inflame the pain and make the problem more difficult than it needs to be. In that case, the proper way to work with it—at least for the time being—will be to avoid thinking about it. Later, when you have regained your composure and mental strength, you should try to resolve the problem or release it through meditation.

However, for those of us with minds that are strong and wild, it will be helpful not only to see our problem, but also to feel and experience the pain deeply. If we are the kind of person who feels that we are almost always right and other people are wrong, our pride can blind us to our problems. So immediately facing pain, rather than avoiding it, can touch the core of your life, bring you back to your senses, and focus your attention in the right direction.

Sometimes avoidance is the best approach for past hurts. Even if you have a residue of pain, the effect may be diminished if the negative experience is followed by a strong positive one. In that case, the problem may be somewhat neutralized. Then, instead of re-creating the problem, it is probably best to just go on with the positive experiences.


## RECOGNITION AND ACCEPTANCE

Sometimes, just by looking at a problem, we can dismiss it at a glance as unimportant and go on with our lives. But other problems need to be faced fully to be healed. This is what the healing exercises are for. But before healing, the first step is recognition and acceptance.

Many people attempt to push away big problems or repress them. We know that grasping makes problems worse, and so does repressing. It is another form of attachment to "self," since we are labeling the problem as something to be avoided at all costs. As long as we cling to this negative view, we constrict our true nature by trying to push away what we don't want. Trying to shove away problems that need to be healed may put them out of sight for a while, but to our dismay they often reappear in a stronger or more poisonous form.

If we do not identify the problem but try to cover it up, it is like trying to perform surgery with our eyes closed. To find a remedy, we need to see and accept the problem clearly for what it is.

At the same time, we do not need to complicate our problem, even if it seems severe, by magnifying the difficulties in our minds. Even if our emotions have upset us, we can use our intellect to tell ourselves that we can deal with the problem. We can remind ourselves that other people have successfully dealt with problems like ours. It might be even more helpful to remember that we have tremendous inner wisdom, strength, and resilience, even if we don't always feel or know this because of our surface afflictions. If we become overly sensitive and emotional about our problems, the wheel of suffering will only turn faster. Shantideva writes:

> Heat, cold, rain, wind, and sickness,
> Bandages, beatings, and so forth,
> To these you should not be sensitive.
> For if you are, the problems they cause will increase.

After recognizing a problem, we need to be ready to do whatever is necessary to remedy it. We should be eager and confident that we can improve our lives. Some people unconsciously, or even consciously, cling to their problems. Some say, "I like turmoil, it adds spice to life," but maybe what they really mean is that they would rather suffer. Our goal should be to heal our suffering.

If we are committed to healing, every problem will become easier to deal with and tolerate, and it is possible that others that we thought permanent and unresolvable will vanish without a trace. We need to be skillful and dedicated, and this is where we can help ourselves by beginning right away, before we are faced with big problems. As Shantideva says:

> If you are trained,
> There is nothing which will not become easy.
> First by training to tolerate minor problems,
> Later you will become able to tolerate great problems.

## FINDING THE SOURCE

While the root of all suffering is grasping at self, we will want to find the particular source of the problem at hand. As an aid to recognizing a problem, this exercise is helpful. Sit in a comfortable place where there are few distractions. Relax your body and mind. Take a couple of deep breaths, and imagine that all your worries are released with the out-breath. Feel peaceful, clear, and spacious. Relax in that peace for a while. Then slowly look at the problem you are facing. See it and also feel it. Acknowledge its presence.

Remember when, where, and how this problem may have begun. In your mind, slowly go back to the earliest possible time, place, and source of the pain. See the possible shape, color, temperature, and location of the problem.

Going back to the original source of problems has several benefits. First, just by contemplating the causes and feeling them, we are already healing. Second, going back through the past produces a greater sense of time and space than we are now aware of, and by opening up to a more spacious and broader perspective we will feel less anxiety about this particular problem. Finally, by going to the root, we can catch the problem naked at its source and uproot it like a weed through the healing exercises.

We don't have to become obsessive about finding and completely understanding the root of every problem; rather, we should work with the cause as it reveals itself at this moment.

Also, we should practice compassion toward ourselves and others in this process. For example, if we find that our parents made mistakes that harmed us, we should clearly see this. At the same time, we should keep in mind that they are subject to ignorance, desire, or hatred like other people, including us. We should feel sympathy for them, and also rejoice in the opportunity to break the chain of ignorance that may have harmed parents and children for many generations in our family. Our reaction could be, "How wonderful that I see this now and can heal a poison that has harmed our family for so long!"

## RELEASING PROBLEMS THROUGH FEELING

In connecting with problems and their source, we should see them objectively—how they appear and what they are—but we shouldn't label them negatively. Otherwise our training could set in motion another cycle of emotions and suffering.

Here is a simple example: If you have a pain in your head, it is good to know what is wrong and what the cause is. Similarly, if you have a problem with a friend, it is good to acknowledge the problem and understand it so that you can start dealing with it. But conceptually and emotionally, if you see and feel the problem as "bad," "terrible," "unbearable," and so forth, then what is a relatively small difficulty will grow into a forest fire. The way to deal with problems emotionally is to say, "I have a headache, but that's OK," or at least, "It's bad, but I can handle it," or, "It's painful, but everyone gets sick at one time or another."

In healing, no emotion is wrong or needs to be denied. We should accept the existence of our feelings, welcome them, and allow them to surface so they can be released. If the training stirs up emotional pain, see it as positive, since the pain indicates that the training is having an impact and that a shaking-up process is taking place. It is okay to feel sad about problems. Allow yourself to feel your sadness and express it as a way of making contact with the root of the problem, to extract the root of pain from your system. If tears come, allow yourself to cry. Crying releases mental stress, physical pressure, and chemical toxins that build up when we hold pain in.

Telling our problems to others who know how to listen also helps relieve pain. It will be more healing for us if we express our thoughts naturally and frankly without grasping, hiding, or defending our pain. If we release the pressure by breathing deeply and crying, that is part of healing too.

We should feel our emotions when they stir, but not get stuck in the pain or let the problem make any stronger impact on us than necessary, sinking deeper roots into our minds and strengthening our negative attitudes and perhaps even our physical symptoms. The idea is to remove the pain, not dig so deep that we harm ourselves. Worrying about our worries makes our problems worse, not better. As Dodrupchen says:

> If we do not feel anxious about problems, our strength of mind can help us to bear even great sufferings easily. We will be able to feel them as being light and insubstantial like cotton. But if we harbor anxiety, it will make even small sufferings intolerable. For example, while we are thinking of the beauty of a girl, even if we try to get rid of desire, we will only be burned. Similarly, if we concentrate on the painful characteristics of suffering, we will not be able to develop tolerance for it.

When we are suffering, we need to open, and not try to force our feelings into some set of rigid expectations. Some problems heal instantly, while others can take a long time. For example, grief can be a very big emotion. We should allow grief its natural space to heal, and not set ourselves a timetable. Trying to hurry grief is like wanting a river to stop to our specifications. The river has to flow along, subside to a trickle, and finally run its course. If we demand a quick fix or deny our grief, it may become submerged in a way that can harm us for years.

# FACING PROBLEMS CALMLY

We need to be balanced in how we deal with problems, especially if other people are involved. If we are under great emotional pressure, it is best not to say or do anything. If you feel angry, excited, or extremely happy, wait a while. Otherwise, what you say will be untrue or partially true, and likely to harm. When you feel more calm, think about your options, what is realistic and what is not. The time to talk things over or make decisions is when we are calm.

In dealing with relationship problems, recognizing a problem is important. But so is the broader perspective in which each person recognizes his or her own faults and mistakes. Instead of igniting an emotional storm, wait until you're calm and clear, when you can think rationally: "What's causing our problem?" When you begin to find it, even if the problem seems difficult, you should recognize it in a relaxed way, thinking, "Yes, this is it. Thank goodness I am close to the cause of the problem!" Without losing the continuity of peace of mind, accept and face the problem with the determination of healing it, thinking: "I am not okay, my partner is not okay, our relationship is not okay, but all that is okay. We will work on it. We can heal it."

At this stage, if you can't avoid the rising of anxiety in your belly, don't worry about the anxiety. If you don't worry about worrying, the worries themselves will lose their sting instead of gathering strength.

## SEEING PROBLEMS AS POSITIVE

If we habitually dwell on and struggle with the negative side of our situation, our whole mentality, perception, and experience will inexorably become negative and filled with suffering. Seeing a problem as negative, constantly thinking and talking about how awful or painful it is, makes even minor problems insurmountably big and solid like a mountain, sharp like a knife, and dark as night. Dodrupchen writes:

> Whenever problems come to us from beings or inanimate objects, if our mind gets used to perceiving only the suffering or the negative aspects of them, then even from a small negative incident great mental pain will ensue. For it is the nature of indulgence in any concept, whether suffering or happiness, that the experience of this happiness or suffering will thereby be intensified. As this negative experience gradually becomes stronger, a time will come when most of what appears before us will become the cause of bringing us unhappiness, and happiness will never have a chance to arise. If we do not realize that the fault lies with our own mind's way of gaining experience, and if we blame all our problems on the external conditions alone, then the ceaseless flame of habitual negative deeds such as hatred and suffering will increase in us. That is called: "All appearances arising in the form of enemies."

Whatever the circumstance, we should try to see its positive aspect, even if it appears to be negative. However, if we have a negative thought or feeling, it is important to be gentle with ourselves. Let us not make the feeling even more negative by saying, "Oh, here I go again," or "What an idiot I am!" If we do, the wheel of negativity will be set in motion endlessly. Instead, we should be aware of our thoughts and feelings, say, "Oh, well," and turn our attention toward the healing exercises, if we can, or something else, redirecting our minds from the negative cycle to the right path. Dodrupchen emphasizes:

> We should not only make our mind impervious to misfortune and suffering, but also bring bliss and peace to our mind from the vicissitudes themselves. For this to happen, we should prevent the arising of the antagonists of evil forces and unharmonious words. We should accustom ourselves to generate only the feeling of liking them. To do this, we should cease to view harmful circumstances as negative and should make every effort to train ourselves to view them as valuable. For whether

things are pleasing or not totally depends on how our mind perceives them.

Strong positive energy can prevent or ease suffering. But the most significant result of a positive attitude is not necessarily to keep suffering from happening, but to keep it from becoming a negative and painful force when it does come. Dodrupchen writes:

> So, to become invincible in the face of obstacles such as ene-mies, illness, and harmful forces as the result of spiritual train-ing does not mean that we can drive them away or that they will not recur. Rather, it means that they will not be able to arise as obstacles to the pursuit of the path of happiness and enlightenment.

We can make friends with our problems. When difficult emotions come, we can ask them what they want. By becoming friendlier to our problems, we can find out what we need to do. We may need to relax and stop grasping, to take better care of ourselves and our true needs, or to change our behavior in some particular way. Problems hold the key to their own healing if we bring our awareness to them, rather than pushing them away or clinging blindly to them. By allowing enough space for a big problem, we are getting ourselves ready to heal.

A major goal of spiritual practice is to clear our mental space of the intellectual and emotional garbage we have been collecting since childhood, and to provide space for the experience of true relaxation and enjoyment. We should realize that a positive thought or inspiration becomes nourishment for the mind, like healthy food. But negative views and passions, like waste prod-ucts, have toxic effects.

So we should see ourselves and our problems clearly, but without dragging ourselves deeper into pain. If we push too hard to solve our problems, we can inflame them. Sometimes it is necessary to be patient and allow problems to unfold and release when they are ready.

Staying balanced and positive is not always easy. So it is very important to make a determined effort not to let our mind dwell on problems as negative. If we can only see our problems negatively, the solution is to occupy our minds with something else, such as reading, gardening, or painting, or the beauty of nature, art, or music.

Our flickering minds need practice in positive attitude, and this comes in how we deal with the details of everyday life. If it is raining out, we can appreciate the rain. Sunny days are beautiful, but rain can be beautiful too. If the rain seems like an inconvenience, put on a raincoat and carry an umbrella, without getting dragged down in negativity. We see the rain as it is, and get on with our lives.

When we make the best of a situation, our mind becomes stronger. When we learn to laugh at ourselves and our problems, we heal. When we learn to enjoy ourselves and refrain from seeing problems as negative, we become more positive about everything. Positive thinking is a wonderful habit to develop, for it heals us and makes us happy in our lives. Dodrupchen explains:

> By practicing this kind of training, our mind will become gentle. Our attitude will become broad. We will become easy to be with. We will have a courageous mind. Our spiritual training will become free from obstacles. All bad circumstances will arise as glorious and auspicious. Our mind will always be satisfied by the joy of peace. To practice the path of enlightenment in this age of dregs we must never be without the armor of this kind of training that turns happiness and suffering into the path of enlightenment. When we are not afflicted by the suffering of anxiety, not only will other mental and emotional sufferings disappear, like weapons dropping from the hands of soldiers, but in most cases, even the actual negative forces, such as illnesses themselves, will also automatically disappear.
>
> The holy ones of the past said: "By not feeling any dislike toward or discontent about anything, our mind will remain un-

disturbed. When our mind is not disturbed, our energy will not get disturbed, and thereby other elements of the body will also not be disturbed. Because of this peace and harmony, our mind will not be disturbed, and so the wheel of joy will keep revolving." They also said: "As birds find it easy to injure horses and donkeys with sores on their backs, negative forces will easily find the opportunity to harm those people whose nature is fearful with negative anxieties. But it will be difficult to harm those whose nature is strong with positive attitude."

When we no longer are so concerned about having to protect and cling to the self, suffering becomes a means of realizing peace and happiness. With positive attitude, suffering can become like candy. In Buddhism, the analogy is made to *ladu*, a sweet but devilishly spicy confection from India. Dodrupchen shows us the tremendous benefits of developing an easygoing tolerance:

> We should think, "Just as the sufferings that I have undergone in the past have greatly helped me to achieve today's happiness in many magnificent forms, . . . which are all difficult to obtain, so too the suffering I am now experiencing will continue to help me to attain these same excellent results. So, even if my suffering is severe it is supremely agreeable." As it is said:
>
> > It is like *ladu* of molasses
> > Mixed with cardamom and pepper.
>
> Think about this again and again, and cultivate the experience of bliss and peace of the mind. Through training in this way, there will arise an overwhelming nature or superabundance of mental bliss, and that makes the sufferings of the sense-faculties as easy as if they were imperceptible. Thus, having a mind that cannot be hurt by suffering is the characteristic of those who overcome illness by tolerance. . . . "Reversing the thought of dislike for suffering" is the foundation of "turning suffering into the path [of enlightenment]." For while our mind is disturbed and our courage and cheerfulness are extinguished by anxiety, we will not be able to turn our suffering into the path.

Of course, many of us would simply like to hide our heads in the sand when suffering comes. If we do not have a great deal of experience in positive attitude, we may wonder how it is possible for anyone to embrace life fully, the negative along with the positive. It is like a sky diver who has learned to float in the vast sky. When we see someone cheerfully at play while falling through the air, we wonder how this is possible. The trick is to relax and let go. After a while, we can become more open to life.

We can begin by broadening our perspective of negative experiences. For example, we usually think of sadness as negative. However, when we properly grieve, it is not really negative, for we are healing from a hurt. In some cases, sadness can actually appear to be quite beautiful. For instance, many people believe that sad songs in opera or popular music are beautiful. So the emotion of sadness is not necessarily "bad" unless we see it as such.

Beyond negative and positive, ultimately all phenomena are open. So because experience is open, we can choose a positive outlook and not feel so anxious even when a situation looks bad. It can also help to see and feel problems as completely open. We can meditate in openness.

## SEEING THE OPENNESS OF YOUR PROBLEMS

When we feel overwhelmed by such problems as sadness or loneliness, we can merge in the openness of the sadness. Allow your breathing to become relaxed. Instead of trying to push the sadness away, or labeling it as something bad, stay where you are mentally, open but calm. Allow the breeze of sadness to come, as if you are welcoming it with open arms. Feel it without grasping or judging, just as it is. Be at ease as much as you can. Slowly experience and taste the feeling of sadness itself.

Relax and merge with the feeling, lose yourself in it, space into space. See and accept it, be at one with it. You have gone beyond the concepts of sadness, and you are with the true nature of the sadness, the ultimate peace. After a while, you may find that the sadness is easier to be with. Perhaps it has begun to dissolve into a peaceful feeling. Relax within that peace as long as you can.

We can deal with physical pain in the same way. Of course, we should use our common sense about pain, and for severe or unusual pain it makes sense to consult a doctor if that is possible. Meditative approaches to pain and suffering do not exclude other therapies and treatments that may be helpful.

In dealing with pain, sometimes it will immediately ease if we don't mind it so much or think of it as negative.

At other times, it may be necessary to fully face it. People with chronic pain may find it eases somewhat if they practice meditating upon it. Merge with the pain. Give yourself a chance to see the pain without the usual label of dislike. In a slow and relaxed way, approach the physical sensation you are feeling, and simply be with it. As you maintain your relaxed breathing, experience the physical sensation. Stay with the sensation in a peaceful way for a long time, or however much time you feel comfortable doing so. Finally, slowly bring your awareness back to the rest of your body and to your surroundings.

You may find that the physical sensation experienced in this way is not as bothersome as usual, and that you can carry this experience into other aspects of your life. It may help to spend some time with the pain every day in this peaceful and gentle way.

The open approach to problems is one of the highest practices of Buddhism, but anyone can use it in daily life, along with the cultivation of positive attitude.


## DEALING WITH FEAR

Many people are troubled by fear and anxiety, and would like to free themselves from emotions that constrict their lives. The remedy for fear, like so many problems, lies within us. Depending on circumstance and temperament, there are many approaches. It may be useful here to discuss a number of them, as a way of reviewing some of the practical skills presented in this book.

Perhaps one of the first realizations to make is that fear can be a friend and helper. In times of danger, fear can give strength to our legs, allowing us to run faster than we ever thought possible. We can also appreciate the more mundane face of fear in everyday life. For example, if we are afraid we will flunk an exam, we might feel motivated to study hard enough to pass it.

If fear or anxiety is a symptom of a deeper problem, we shouldn't cover it up. By being attentive to an anxiety that seems compelling and sharp, we may find the key to a problem that we can then go about healing.

Often we can simply face fear and it will go away. After all, fear and anxiety are created within our minds. Knowing that these emotions are fabrications can empower us to banish them. When anxiety has become a habit, a negative pattern of thought, we should remind ourselves that it is not real or solid. We may think anxiety is real because of our habitual grasping at it, but if we relax that grip, it may surprise us to discover that fear is a paper tiger after all.

So we can face fear and find the healing key within it. Or we are free to ignore or dismiss fear. Or we can avoid fear when it seems too big to handle at the moment, and come back to heal it later when we're ready.

Sometimes we can't avoid fear because of circumstances that seem to press in on us. Then we can try to understand fear in its true nature, without the negative label, as pure energy. Good actors and public speakers know that stage fright can make them alert and ready to give an inspired performance. Soldiers who have won medals for bravery in battle report that they felt fear, but the fear was transformed into courage. If we were to merge into the experience, tremendous fear could make us feel fully alive even if we only had a few minutes left on earth. Whatever the situation, the key is not to grasp at fear.

## RELEASING STRONG FEARS

People develop all sorts of phobias, like claustrophobia or fear of flying. In these cases, the problem is fear of fear, the tightening grip of the mind magnifying and multiplying some original fear until the mouth dries up, the throat closes, and the body shakes. The practical way to deal with acute fears gives us a broader lesson about how we can train ourselves to deal with any difficulty.

Let's look at one example, agoraphobia, which means "fear of the marketplace" and is experienced as fear of spaces and public areas. The fear seems so real that people sometimes become prisoners in their homes.

The solution is to see, at first on a conceptual level, that being afraid of fear is a phantom that we can gently train ourselves to overcome. Meditation and positive visualization can help.

We can also use the experience of daily life to train our mind and body in releasing the phobia. The training should be in small steps that are easy enough to handle. At first, walk a short distance out the front door, however far it takes before fear comes. Welcome the fear. Relax your body and breathing, and allow the fear to rise up. Experience the fear; try to be open to it. Remind yourself, "This is just my fearful self. I can let go of this fear." If your body shakes, don't try to force it to stop. Allow the shaking, let go of the wish to push this away, but at the same time maintain a relaxed body and breathing. Let fear go right through you; this is the way to release it. Let fear do its worst, knowing you will survive and that it cannot harm you even though it may seem solid and painful.

When you survive your fear, celebrate this, even if you felt very afraid and continue to fear going places. Rejoice in whatever progress you make. Each day go a bit farther, but also rest sometimes from your training. Acccpt setbacks, when you have to step back out of fear, as part of the journey forward. Encourage yourself constantly, and one day you will be able to go all the way to some place you have picked as a goal. Reward yourself, perhaps by buying a treat or simply reveling in being there. After this great victory, keep practicing your new skill. Fortify your strength until you are totally free of fear.

This approach is used in modern behavioral psychology as a remedy for phobias, and it is also in accordance with Buddhist spiritual practices. Those of us fortunate enough not to have this particular phobia will recognize the universality of the technique and its relevance to our own lives and spiritual practice.

We need to take small steps, encourage ourselves, and practice consistently. We are human and need help with our afflictions. The greatest source of help and strength is our minds—we can call upon the healing power within us. This is the purpose of the healing exercises, which will help us deal with fear and our other problems.

# 6

# HOW TO DEAL WITH PHYSICAL AILMENTS ~

FOR MANY OF US, the ills of the body are like a magnet for our anxieties. We sometimes feel our ailments as reminders of how finite and fragile we humans are. This is not necessarily bad, for a whiff of mortality can give us a better appreciation for the here and now. Even the minor sickness of a head cold can help us practice the letting go of self, and in so doing grant us the freedom to make the most of every part of our lives.

Although physical sickness can be harder to remedy through the power of the mind than emotional problems, the mind nonetheless does have a great role in physical healing. In some cases, the mind alone can heal physical sickness, even where conventional medicine has failed.

Buddhism draws very little distinction between the sickness of the mind and body. In fact, the *Four Tantras*, the ancient canon of Tibetan medicine, declares that all sickness is the result of grasping at self. The *Shedgyud*, one of these tantras, says:

> The general cause of sickness,
> The sole cause of all the sicknesses,

Is the unenlightenment of not realizing the true nature of
no-self.
For example, a bird will never be separated from its shadow
Even if it is flying in the sky [and the shadow is invisible];
Likewise, people who are unenlightened will never be free
from sickness,
Even if they are remaining in and enjoying happiness.

The specific causes of sickness are that unenlightenment
produces
Desire, hatred, and ignorance,
And they produce the ills of air, bile, and phlegm as the result.

Zurkharpa Lodrö Gyaltshen, commenting on the ancient
texts on medicine, writes:

Medicine is a synonym for healing.
It is healing of the afflictions of air [energy], bile, and phlegm
of the body,
It is the healing of the afflictions of desire, hatred, and
ignorance of the mind.

If you are healthy in your mind, it often follows that your
body will be healthy too. However, even deeply spiritual people
get sick. How do we explain this?

The Buddha realized total enlightenment, beyond suffering
and the laws of cause and effect known as karma. But the Buddha
was also human. Like all of us, he had a body that was subject to
decay and death. Yet one who is enlightened has released grasping
at self and so does not experience sickness as suffering. It is the
attitude of the mind that counts the most.

Even for those of us who are not yet realized spiritually, the
more we can relax, the less severe our sickness will seem. This is
the practical lesson we all can understand and take to heart. With
a positive attitude you won't feel as bad, and your body will be
better able to heal itself.

It may sound strange, but we can actually welcome sickness

when it comes. Buddhists see sickness as a broom that sweeps away the accumulations of negative attitudes and emotions. Jigme Lingpa writes:

> There is no better fuel than sicknesses to burn off bad karma.
> Don't entertain a sad mind or negative views over sicknesses,
> But see them as signs of the waning of your bad karma, and
>     rejoice over them.

For non-Buddhists and Buddhists alike, sickness can provide an opportunity to slow down, let go, and appreciate life even in the midst of suffering.

Sometimes when your body begins feeling out of balance, you can release the sickness before it takes root by being very restful in mind and body. But if in spite of this you do come down with a cold or the flu, don't mind too much. Try not to feel victimized, as if the flu bug had singled you out! Lots of people are sick, and by remembering this you can put your own suffering in perspective and develop compassion for the human family to which you belong.

Everything is impermanent, including sickness, even when it seems as if you will feel bad forever. Remember that the bad feeling will eventually go away.

When you are sick, try to find something to feel good about. Meditate while lying in bed, or read an inspiring book. Or if you feel too sick at the moment for that, with simplicity and appreciation you can gaze out the window, watch the pattern of light within your room, or listen to the sounds of activity outside. If you feel miserable with some symptom like nausea, don't anticipate that in the next moment you might feel more pain or misery. Abide calmly in your body, and simply be with the feeling in as relaxed a way as possible. If you must spend time in a sickroom, you could bring some inspiring object like a picture or flower near you to provide comfort.

You should take good care of yourself and your health. This

advice is so utterly obvious; why is it that some of us ignore it? Even something as simple as taking a bath when we are exhausted can be very caring and comforting. Some people are reckless with their health. Others mistakenly believe that taking care of themselves is somehow selfish. But this attitude is grasping at the "self" of so-called selflessness. The right attitude is to love ourselves, without grasping. First we must know what true self-love is, for otherwise how can we ever love others?

When people fall seriously ill, their spirit may plunge. They may feel helpless. They may blame themselves for causing their own sickness or be persuaded by others who tell them that it is their own fault.

Blame has no place in healing. If you can find something in your lifestyle that has directly caused the illness, this is good. Then your attitude should be: "I've been mischievous in my behavior, but now I have the motivation to change!" However, while grasping at self is the ultimate cause of suffering and sickness, the law of karma tells us that there can be an infinite number of causations for any single event—and we may not be able to identify all of them. If may be enough to simply acknowledge that we are human, and now we are sick. The right attitude is to get on with healing.

If possible, don't be too solemn about sickness—even serious illness. When doom and gloom descend, that could be a terrific moment for a joke! If you can be playful when the stakes are very high, your courage can inspire you and everyone else. I had a Tibetan friend in India who brought joyful peals of laughter to his friends with everything he said and did. One day he got into a car accident in Darjeeling. When his friends rushed into his hospital room, he was in no position to crack jokes. Still, although he was delighted to see his friends, he pretended to be upset, turning his face away from them. Immediately, loud laughter filled the room, as his friends recognized that he was teasing them, and an air of life and ease prevailed.

Take a wise and reasoned approach to deciding the best

treatment, and be open to any approach that can help. This could certainly include conventional medicine. Sometimes people who are interested in taking up meditation think they should refuse medications or the benefits of modern science, under the misguided impression that they must rely solely on their mind rather than anything external. But even the most advanced healers of Tibetan Buddhism prescribe the "external material" of medicines. There is nothing wrong with taking pills if they can help us.

Balance comes in handy when we are sick. Don't push yourself if you need to rest in bed; just let go. On the other hand, even for severe illness, don't take too seriously the limits on wellness imposed by others, or self-imposed. It can be surprising how soon even after surgery we can begin to move about. A mind that is well and positive will speed recovery from any sickness. The mind can be like a general whose fearless attitude turns his defeated troops around and leads them to victory.

If you feel isolated by sickness, come out of yourself. Make an effort to connect with friends, family, or anyone around you. Get up and rejoin the world. This is excellent medicine. Even if you can't get up or are in pain, pick up the phone and talk to somebody—a friend, a relative, a clergy person or social worker. If you can, read an inspiring book, listen to refreshing music, look at the beauty of flowers or a painting, see the beauty of light coming in the window. If you can't look at anything inspiring, think of someone or something you love and enjoy it. If your mind is enjoying, you are on the path of healing. Also, you could think about other people who are sick. Imagine that your suffering is making theirs bearable, that somehow you can lift theirs away entirely just by taking their worries and folding them into your pain. This is a Buddhist meditation of compassion that anyone can use. It can lighten the burden of your own emotions. In some cases, its power to release could actually help to heal your physical problem.

Be kind to anger, fear, or discouragement if they arise, no

matter if they are strong or persistent, for a patient approach can allow even the most turbulent emotions to become healing energy. If you are impatient, see even that as positive, for it means you want to get better.

This attitude of kindness can extend even to the sickness that is in your body until it can be healed. In Buddhism, the body is considered a heavenly pure land. One Buddhist meditation honors the very bacteria (or "insects," as Tibetans think of them) that are normal within a healthy body. If we have an unhealthy virus or infection, the goal is to heal it, but we don't need to recoil from it or feel tainted. We can acknowledge that a dangerous sickness is sharing our body, without becoming overly identified with it.

Many of us dread as a worst-case scenario being trapped in a body that is too sick or injured to move. Yet think how many people with disabilities are able to rise above even this limitation through a positive attitude. A famous example is Stephen Hawking, an eminent British astrophysicist, whose enthusiasm for the life of the mind transcends the total paralysis of his body and inability to speak. A friend of mine, the Reverend Nellie Greene, also has severe neurological damage but a clear mind and, through an attitude of perseverance, has become a deacon in the Episcopal Church. So while the body can be very ill, the mind doesn't have to be.

Not every sickness can be cured or "fixed." After all, the body is but a guest house, where we dwell for our allotted time but finally have to leave. We all die. But even if we only have a few months or days to live, we can see even terminal illness as an opportunity. To know that we are dying could be a real blessing, for then we could fully grieve for ourselves and open in a way that we may have found difficult when our health was robust. We can tell those dear to us how much we love them, and mend relationships that may have become strained. We can find value in the small moments of life that we have.

Death itself can be a profound healing. Even if the condition leading to one's death is very difficult or physically painful, peace is possible. Everything in life, including dying, can be a letting go.

But don't let go of life too soon! Treasure the precious gift of your life, and if there is a chance to live, be firmly determined that you can and will get better. In the natural order of things, the Lord of Death has eventual mastery over the body. When Death calls, we must go: this is how it is. Yet sometimes we can cheat Death a bit—we don't have to answer his call right away.

When I was studying at the Scripture College at Dodrup-chen monastery, there was a classmate of mine named Chöjor. He was a gentle, cheerful, and studious young monk who suffered from severe epilepsy. Every few months, sometimes several times a day, he would go through violent epileptic fits. His convulsions brought serious fear and disruption into his life and utter chaos into our classes and ceremonies.

Eventually, a senior lama called Tulku Jiglo, had a solution. He was round and very jolly, like the popular figure of the Chinese laughing Buddha. Though he didn't have a single tooth left, he was always smiling broadly as he joked and teased people—all while saying his unceasing prayers. Tulku knew a special prayer known to cure epilepsy. With an empowerment ceremony, he transmitted this knowledge to Chöjor and a group of us. From that day for a whole month, every evening just before sunset, we had to do a half-hour prayer with a simple cake offering. The prayer consists of a ceremony of making offerings to planets or celestial bodies in the context of Buddhist meditation. Tibetans believe that epilepsy is caused by planetary influences. Since then, for as long as I knew him, Chöjor was free from epileptic attacks. Such healing takes place as the result of opening one's mind with positive attitude, inviting the healing power from energy sources (in this case from planets), and believing in the healing effects. This is healing, not through material means, but through spiritual and mental powers.

It isn't only Tibetan spiritual masters or monks who can

recover from dire sickness. A good friend of mine survived what was supposed to be a fatal disease through meditation, and his case is not so unusual. Harry Winter was seventy-four years old in 1988 when he was diagnosed with lung cancer. He was given six months to live, but as an experienced meditator Harry had great faith that his mind could at the very least slow the disease. In addition to meditation aimed at relaxing his mind and removing any mental obstructions, he began a healing visualization half an hour each day.

He had surgery twice, confounding doctors with both his survival and the remission of his cancer. When the disease returned after five years, he refused a third operation that would have left him bedridden. He continued to meditate daily and deeply, bringing feelings of peace and warmth into the rest of the day. During one period, he meditated eight hours a day.

On his eightieth birthday, Harry was completely free of cancer and in better overall physical health than he had been six years before, to the astonishment of his doctors. The harvest of so much meditation also left him with a deepened spiritual richness.

The meditation Harry used involved visualizing healing nectar from Vajrasattva, the Buddha of Purification. In his mind, he would see the deity at the crown of his head, and nectar streaming down into his own body. Harry thought of the nectar as "helpers" that touched and healed the cancerous cells of his body, and also purified all emotional defilements. Harry's meditation always included his wish for purification of *all* beings and the entire universe. The healing exercises that Harry followed are one of the main principles that this book teaches in the following chapters.

# 7

# HEALING ENERGIES 〜

## THE SOURCE OF POWER

For most healing meditations, it is very important to rely on a blessing or energy from a "source of power" as an aid in transforming suffering.

The source of power is a tool—a skillful means—that can arouse the energy and wisdom within us for healing. A Buddhist could use the image, presence, and blessing energy of a spiritual divinity, such as the Buddha. Others might rely on any vision of God or sacred image according to their own belief. The source of power could be any positive form, nature, essence, or force— the sun, moon, space, water, a river, the ocean, air, fire, trees, flowers, people, animals, light, sound, smell, taste—any aspect of energy that one finds inspiring and healing. For example, one could visualize in the sky a bright, pure, shining ball of light and imagine it as the pure essence of the universe and the embodiment of all healing energies.

Generally, forms of spiritual beings (such as a Buddha, the Blessed Virgin, Lord Krishna, or the Mother Goddess) are more effective than ordinary forms, as they express and embody the ultimate peace and joy of the universal truth. However, the best source of power for you is the one that you yourself feel most comfortable with: any visualized image or presence that inspires warmth, peace, and positive energy.

After determining a source of power, it is important to spend many days, before we begin to train in this meditation, reflecting upon the source of power and establishing a link with its energy. Later, when practicing the actual healing exercises (as explained in the second part of this book), we should renew the connection to its energy by visualizing, experiencing, and trusting it.

If imagining a particular source of power causes tightness, narrowness, and stress, then even if it is a true divine object, we are regarding it in the wrong way, with a mind of attachment based on confusion and self-grasping, and it will not help us ease our problems. On the other hand, even when we have found something that feels right for us, it is okay to change it, depending on our needs and spiritual or emotional growth.

When we connect with the source of power we should feel and embrace the peace and energy it gives us. With the right attitude, any object can become tremendously powerful. Paltrül Rinpoche tells this story:

> A woman of great devotion asked her son, who frequently went to India on business, to bring her a sacred object from the land of Buddha—India. The son forgot about it until he got close to home. He took a tooth from the corpse of a dog, wrapped it up in brocade and silk, and handed it to his mother, saying, "Mother, I brought a tooth of the Buddha to be the object of your homage." For the rest of her life the mother worshiped the tooth with total belief and devotion as if it were a true tooth of the Buddha. From the tooth miraculous signs appeared, and at the time of her death rainbow lights arched over her body as a sign of high spiritual attainment.

Some people may think they are too sophisticated to rely on an image to help them. They may feel that any image or visualization would be something "made up" that is external to themselves; but on the contrary, the use of imagery actually helps us to draw upon untapped strength that we already possess. What we choose as the form or image of the source of power doesn't matter so much, because it is really our own inner wisdom that we are contacting. What matters is our confidence in and openness to this wisdom, as a celebration of the true nature of the universe. In cultivating a source of power, we ease the narrow, rigid attitudes and feelings that are creating many problems for us, and develop a positive mind that is open to healing.

If the source of power brings a feeling of warmth, peace, and strength to us when we visualize it, we have made it ours. Now we can apply its power to heal our emotional, mental, and spiritual difficulties, and to develop strength of mind.

## LIGHT AS A MEANS OF HEALING

In addition to meditating upon a source of power, we can also use our imagination to visualize various manifestations of earth, air, fire, water, space, or light as a way to bring blessings and healing energies to ourselves. For example, we can see and feel the power of earth to stabilize and strengthen. Air can sweep, clean, and inspire. Fire can warm, transform, refine, and empower. If a particular problem seems to call for a cooling of our emotions, we can imagine the soothing, purifying power of water.

Of all these elemental powers, light is the most vital means prescribed in the Buddhist scriptures for healing and receiving blessings.

We all know intuitively that light is a positive force, and on an empirical level we can see how important light is in nature and our surroundings. Light makes the crops and vegetation of the earth grow. We can observe how houseplants follow the light, turning their leaves toward its nourishment. A beautiful sunny day feels like a blessing even to people who don't consider themselves religious, and office workers are happier when they sit near a window where they can be aware of daylight and the openness of the outdoors.

Spiritually, light is central to many traditions, celebrated at festivals and other commemorations with candles, decorative lamps, or sacred fires. Light is associated with divinity in several faiths. For example, in the Hindu *Bhagavad Gita*, the Lord is revealed as a being of overwhelming radiance. And in the New Testament, Jesus Christ proclaims, "I am the light of the world."

In the Buddhist view, light can be understood on two levels—the relative and the absolute. We can see the relative forms of light in the natural world, feel the warmth of light, observe and measure it with instruments.

Beyond relative light is the absolute light or Buddha light of oneness and openness. We can gain some understanding of light in the absolute from the stories that people have told of their near-death experiences—of merging and being at one with a radiant light, with no sense of self separate from the peace and joy of this extraordinary light. Despite our attempts to describe it, absolute light transcends the limitations of space, time, measurement, or concepts. It is inseparable from the enlightened mind and total openness.

According to the esoteric teachings of Nyingma Buddhism, all of nature is an expression of absolute light. However, because of our grasping at self and the dualistic perceptions that arise from this grasping—the notion of an "I" separate from my surroundings, of "subject" distinct from "object"—nature appears before us as solid and separate. Quoting an ancient tantric text, *The Golden Rosary (gSer Phreng)*, Kunkhyen Longchenpa gives a mystical description of the five "pure lights" of Buddha wisdom in their mundane appearance:

> Due to grasping at the "self,"
> Of blue, white, yellow, red, and green lights,
> They have spontaneously appeared as the five gross elements
> Of space, water, earth, fire, and air.

Although these teachings about light may be interesting to Buddhists, they do not need to be a big concern for anyone whose main focus is the everyday healing of the mind. The point to understand is that light can be a great source of healing and joy, one that has a practical use in meditation to ease our problems.

In the healing exercises drawn from Buddhist teachings, whatever vivid and inspiring images of light we are able to visualize can help us, even if we perceive of light as relative rather than absolute. Since in most people's concept light tends to be expansive and open, meditating on light can relax our grasping at self and bring us the feeling of peace and openness.

## VISUALIZING LIGHT

Always when we call upon light, or any other means of healing, we need to visualize an image or presence, to feel its positive qualities, and to believe in its power to heal. Be creative in imagining light in a way that works for you. As you practice, you may find that your ability to meditate upon light deepens and strengthens.

You might find it helpful to imagine light showering down upon you, suffusing and radiating your mind and body with its healing warmth, bringing openness and relaxation to everything it touches. Or you could imagine light coming from your source of power. Perhaps the light takes the form of rainbow-colored beams. Feel that it is filling your mind and body completely, bringing bliss, peace, and health that instantly warms and heals problem areas, or melts them into light and peace. Every part of your body, down to the last cell, is effortlessly filled with light. Then feel that your body is transformed into a body of light, or perhaps a glowing, warm flame if that image is helpful.

At times, you may feel the need for emotional security and protection. Then you could imagine light as an aura or tent around your body, or light that is like a protective eggshell. Such images should make you feel relaxed and open, even while protected. If you feel tight or encased, or cut off and isolated from the world and other people, then try to open up this meditation, or relax and do something else.

Meditations on light can be used to heal specific problems, or they can help generally to make us feel more open and spacious. As we meditate on light, we can imagine the light as expanding beyond our bodies and shining forth without end. We can see the whole world as touched, suffused, and transformed into pure and peaceful light. If we meditate on light in a very open way, we realize that light is infinite, without borders or the limits of time and space.

According to our needs, we can see healing light in a variety of forms. If you have a difficult emotion that seems lodged in some particular area, like your chest or throat, you could place your hand there in a healing and caring way. Just by gently touching, rubbing, or massaging the area as you breathe in a very relaxed way, you can ease your problem. In addition, you could visualize healing light in multiple colors coming from your hand. A contemporary Christian mystic, Omraam Mikhaël Aïvanhov, advises:

> When you are in great pain, ask the light to help you. Imagine that from your fingers emanate rays of light of every color and train these rays on the painful area. You will soon feel a gradual release from the pain.

For some people, meditating upon light creates too much of a sense of flying or floating. If this happens to you, ground yourself by imagining that although the healing light is pure, clear, and universal, its unchanging and unmoving nature makes it feel heavy.

## AWAKENING HEALING ENERGY

All of us possess blazing physical and spiritual energy, in greater abundance than we realize. We can awaken this energy for use in meditation and daily life. Ultimately energy and light are the same. To promote our well-being, mental or physical, we can ignite and magnify our inner energy, light, and wisdom.

As an exercise to awaken this power, meditate on your body as a source of tremendous energy. Sit somewhere comfortable and warm, with eyes closed or half closed. Breathe naturally and calmly. Slowly imagine your body as an amazing, wonderful thing, with its skin, bones, muscles, nerves, and other organs, and its billions of cells of every sort needed for the miracle of life.

You can picture all this with as much scientific accuracy as you want, although a literal approach isn't necessary. For the healing power of the meditation, the key is to use whatever imagery helps you to feel and believe that your body is a positive place of vast energy and resilience.

It can be very helpful to begin by imagining one cell of your body, to enter into that cell, and to see and feel its wondrous vitality. Imagine its vastness. It could be as big as the entire universe.

You might find it helpful to bring certain elemental qualities of earth, air, fire, and water into this contemplation—such as the fertility or strength of the earth, or the cleansing purity of air. You might also appreciate the richness and beauty of this one cell by imagining music or some other peaceful sound, or by touching the cell and feeling it as alive or pulsing with strength.

After devoting some time to this one cell, or two or three cells, gradually broaden your meditation to feel the vastness of your body, its amazing strength and ability to heal. Feel that you are in a place of beauty, wonder, and infinite richness.

Then go back and see one cell, or several cells, as bright and glowing with light. Feel the warmth of the light. Celebrate this peaceful, wonderful place of light, perhaps by again imagining glorious music or sound. Open your meditation up to include your entire body as glowing or even blazing with health and warmth.

Then imagine and feel that any darkness, coldness, pain,

pressure, sorrow, or disharmony in your body or mind is healed by the glowing light, the feelings of peacefulness, the sounds of celebration. All the cells are alive in a communion of warmth and bliss. The healing energy and light of billions of cells, like the rays of billions of suns, fills your body. Return to this feeling again and again, resting and basking in it.

Finally, you could imagine the light and energy as blazing forth from your body, like a bright bonfire in the darkness. You might imagine rays emanating from your body in an aura, a protective circle of healing energy. Then the healing energy expands to touch other people or places, suffusing them in light and peace. Gradually, if you are an experienced meditator, this energy could open to the entire universe. Whatever your contemplation, end by relaxing and being at one with your feelings.

Another exercise to awaken healing energy is to visualize yourself as a divine presence, such as a Buddha or some other wonderful being. Imagine the divinity in yourself, the perfect wisdom within you, and call upon that wisdom to come forth in the form of energy and strength.

## HEALING LIGHT AND ENERGY IN DAILY LIFE

We can incorporate an awareness of light and energy into every part of our lives. This awareness can turn our ordinary lives into a cycle of healing.

A good practice for anyone, no matter what his or her temperament or skill at meditation, is to appreciate the light of nature—the sunshine, the subtle shifts of light during the day and at different seasons of the year, the beautiful sunsets, the moonlight and starlight, the soft glow of an overcast day.

We could also cultivate an awareness of pure, absolute light in our everyday world, at least conceptually. As we move through our daily routine, any awareness of universal light can give us confidence and strength.

So when you sit, don't just sit like a piece of rock. Sit in a relaxed but alert way, with a feeling that celebrates light and energy, as if you were a candle flame radiating light.

When you think, do not think with a confused, grasping, or hateful mind. Be aware that the light of the mind can inspire the clarity of openness and peace.

When you talk, speak with a voice that is neither harsh nor weak. Like light and energy, your voice can be strong, clear, and soothing.

When you walk, do not walk like a puppet of flesh, nerves, and bones, pulled in various directions by the strings of fascination or desire. If you feel the presence of healing light and energy, then you can walk in a way that celebrates this. Instead of merely plodding here and there, through an awareness of light you can endow your movements with energy and grace. Enjoy the expansive feeling of being alive, and open your body in a straight, relaxed posture. Breathe freely and let the energy shine forth. Without exaggerating your movements, feel that you are unencumbered by the weight of worry. You may notice a subtle but joyful bounce in your step, like an astronaut effortlessly walking on the moon.

When you touch, do not touch an object like a robot reaching for a tool. Reach out to it as if healing energy is emanating from your hand, touching an object that is itself a source of light.

Light is not only within us, but everywhere around us. Even though the absolute light of oneness is beyond concepts or images, we can feel or imagine light in its relative form as subtly visible in the air around us and in our everyday surroundings. All of your movements and thoughts can be in communion with a world of light. Even a movement of your finger can be the play, enjoyment, and celebration of light and energy.

As with meditation upon light, the awareness of light in daily life can sometimes result in an uneasy or floating sensation. Then you should imagine the light in your body, or just your feet, as heavy light. Feel that your body is heavy enough not to float and that your feet are firmly touching solid ground.

We should recognize whether a particular exercise is suitable for our personality and capabilities. Some of us might have difficulty being in touch with our true feelings, and we may not be ready for this daily life practice. If you feel tight and closed, you are doing this practice the wrong way. If you feel giddy or manic, turn to a more calming practice or simply do something else.

Students of meditation often ask me whether a particular healing exercise is "right for me" or if they are doing it "the right way." Always, we should do what makes us feel relaxed and open, this is our guide.

Awareness of light is one way to arouse healing energy. There are so many others. Physical activity is a great way to bring balance to our lives and call forth energy. Walking, doing hatha yoga or other exercises, dancing, or singing—these all celebrate life and bring health.

# PART TWO

# THE
# HEALING
# EXERCISES

# 8

# HEALING MEDITATIONS ⁓

## INTRODUCTION

Some of the exercises that follow are taken directly from Tibetan
Buddhist scriptures, while others are elaborated by the author
based on principles taught in the scriptures. Choose whichever
exercise is appropriate for your situation.

To immerse yourself in a healing exercise, you need to be
familiar with the healing tools given in Part One that are applica-
ble to the particular exercise.

Most of these exercises are made up of four basic steps: (1)
recognizing the problems that need to be healed, (2) relying on a
source of power, (3) applying the means of healing, and (4) attain-
ing the result of healing. In some exercises the source of power is
not introduced. Also, in some exercises no image is directly given,
but you may visualize any image that is appropriate.

To make healing truly effective, we need to involve our
power of imagination, our understanding, our feelings, and our
power of belief in the healing process. The more we see, understand, feel, and believe in the healing process, the deeper its
benefits.

We can strengthen each of the four basic healing steps

through four meditation techniques. We could (1) see or visualize each as an image, (2) think of each with its name or designation, (3) feel the qualities of each, and (4) believe in its effectiveness. These techniques are based on the understanding that thoughts gain power as they take a concrete shape in our mind. Seeing makes things vivid and immediate to us. When we name something, we empower it and relate it to ourselves through the power of thought. When we feel something, we become wholly absorbed in it. When we believe in the power and effectiveness of something, it becomes a reality.

For example, to heal sadness, we should apply the four meditation techniques to the four basic steps. First, see the sadness as an image. Realistically and calmly recognize the sadness. Allow the sad feeling or emotion to come up, so that you can then release it. It can sometimes help—although it is not necessary—to locate a place in your body where the sad feeling is concentrated, such as your head, throat, chest, or the pit of your stomach. Perhaps your entire body seems tense. Wherever the sadness is, you can see (visualize) the sadness as an image, such as a block of ice. This enables your mind to touch this unhealthy point with healing energies.

Visualizing, feeling, naming, and believing—but not dwelling—in the reality of our sickness helps us get hold of what is wrong so that we can then cure it directly.

See the source of power in a form, such as a ball of light like the sun, which has the qualities of heat, bliss, and boundlessness.

See the means of healing in the form of powerful beams of fiery light that melt the ice of sadness in your body by their mere touch, like the hot rays of the sun on ice.

See that you are filled with light and then transformed into a brilliant healing light body of warmth, bliss, joy, and openness.

Second, besides seeing these images, we should also name and recognize the sadness, the source of power, the means of healing, and the attainment of healing.

Third, don't just see and name them, but also feel the sadness, without dwelling on it.

Feel the presence of the source of power.

Feel the energy of the means of healing, by invoking the healing energy and tailoring the form of this energy to your needs and situation. It might be a great cleansing wind that sweeps away afflictions, or a nurturing, soothing rain, or the energy of light, or the purifying power of fire—or any other means of healing that is suitable to you.

Feel that you are totally filled with the healing energy of warmth, bliss, joy, strength, and openness.

Then, without further thoughts or images, simply relax and open up to whatever feelings you are having at the end of the exercise.

Finally, don't just see, designate, and feel, but also have complete belief and trust that your sadness *is* in the ice-like image. That the source of power *is* present in front of you with the absolute power to heal. That the means of healing *can* heal you by its mere touch. And that you *are* totally healed and transformed into a healing light body of warmth, bliss, joy, and openness. Feel and believe that your problem is being healed. Take delight in the healing as you see and feel it happen. Believe that your difficulty is soothed, purified, swept away, dispelled. Then, without thoughts or images, simply relax and open up to whatever feelings you are having at the end of the exercise.

Some problems will vanish immediately without a trace. Others may take many sessions.

Also, we should be realistic about the extent of our ability to improve the world around us or change some problems that come our way. However, although meditation may not always change the circumstances we find ourselves in, our attitudes toward them can change. We can be more peaceful and happy. This in itself will improve the situation or change how others around us act.

In the context of the healing exercises, it's important to believe in the power of the meditation to bring us peace. We should give ourselves completely to the exercise and feel as strongly as possible that the problem has totally disappeared. Do not worry about whether the actual situation appears to be difficult to heal. During the time of the meditation, do not concern yourself with anything except the arousing of healing energy and belief in its power. This is the way to awaken the inner strength of mind and body.

As we begin on the healing path in daily life, it's best to deal with a simple problem, such as changing the habit of worrying about the weather or talking too much without thinking. Likewise, when doing healing meditations, it's easier at first to solve one simple problem, rather than many complicated ones. This simple approach generates the skill, habit, and inspiration to gradually deal with bigger ones.

If you are applying a healing exercise for a specific difficulty over many sessions, it may not be necessary to begin each time by feeling or visualizing the image of the problem. After a while, you can begin meditating immediately on the healing energy.

Also think about the sadness and try to determine its character. It can help if you are able to feel whether it is hot or cold. If it is cold, visualize warm light, water, or air as the means of healing. If heat is the problem, visualize cool light, water, or air. Do whatever feels right, and if temperature does not seem to apply, then practice whatever is natural for you.

Remember, too, that if you are already feeling positive, this is the time to deepen your sense of well-being through meditation, and so be ready for troubles when they come. You could contemplate light or your source of power, or use any healing technique. Whatever your practice of healing, always cultivate your meditation as an oasis of peace.

## CLEARING ENERGY BLOCKS

### 1. *Releasing the Shackles of Tension*

We'll begin with a commonsense approach that is helpful by itself or as a preliminary to meditation or any activity.

Concentrating energy and then relaxing is a good way to release any physical or mental tension. Concentrate your mind, feel the tension, and then let go. This is a simple way to release energy blocks in the mind and body.

When you feel stressed, first concentrate on feeling where the pressure is. Often you can release the stress simply by bringing awareness to it, and letting go. If muscles are tense in a certain place, they will relax once awareness of letting go is there.

Release the stress or worry in your head by relaxing the muscles of your face and forehead, and by letting go of all tension. You could also imagine that a healing light is opening up and relaxing the tightness or pain in your head, or wherever it is tense.

Another simple release is to stretch your arms high over your head and tense your hands into fists. Breathe in as you stretch, clench your muscles, hold the position for a moment, then release as you breathe out. A good loud yawn can help you during the release. Feel that all tensions are released as your fists open and let go. If it is helpful, imagine your out-breath as a warm wind that sweeps away the stress. Release the breath into the welcoming infinity of space.

Whatever small step we take to feel less tense can help us a great deal if our attitude is positive and we give ourselves wholly to the release.

## 2. *Restoring the Energy of Peace and Joy*

The source of power, as described in the previous chapter, is a basic means of healing. By calling upon this image, we can provide ourselves with ready comfort when our mind or body is exhausted and life seems hollow, hopeless, and without meaning.

Relax for a couple of minutes. Take some deep breaths, expelling negative or dead energies as you exhale. Now visualize the source of power, and rest your mind and full attention there. Do not rush or become too pushy in the visualization. Rather, allow the positive and relaxed feelings that the image invokes in you to rise up. Slowly build a confident perception that this image is the embodiment of all the positive energy or divinities of the whole universe. Stay with the image, giving yourself wholly to it. Dwell in the feelings of warmth and joy it generates, and rejoice in any positive feelings that come. Finally, let go of images, relax, and be present within your feelings.

### 3. *Nursing the Flower of Positive Energy*

Meditation on a beautiful image in nature, such as a flower, can awaken our joy at being alive. To clear energy blocks, or to reinforce positive energy we are feeling at the moment, imagine a flower just before it buds. Think of yourself as the flower. Either see it right in front of you, or actually feel that your body itself is the flower. Now the flower bud is nurtured with soft rain, sunlight, and a life-giving breeze. Feel these blessings deeply. If it helps, see them as coming from your source of power.

Take your time dwelling upon the bud as it blossoms into an enchanting flower. Its beauty and purity delight all beings. Enjoy the lovely, expansive feelings that such a meditation can evoke.

To extend this exercise into your daily life, when planting, growing, and nurturing plants, imagine that you are sharing and are part of the rich life of the natural world.

When you happen to behold a beautiful image, in daily life, try not to mentally grasp at it as an object "out there," separate from you, or be emotionally attached to it as a sensual commodity. Allow yourself to see the image and feel the experience of beauty with a relaxed and open mind. Then the freshness, openness, joy, and peace—the qualities you are seeing—will blossom in you. The truth is that the concept of beauty and its effects arise in your own mind, not in the objects.

## HEALING OUR EMOTIONS

### 1. *Letting Go of the Dark Cloud of Sadness*

When sadness is strong, acknowledge its presence. Greet it with open arms. Feel the sadness briefly and fully, long enough to embrace it and know the emotion for what it is. By feeling sadness, we can let it go.

Visualize sadness as a dark cloud in your head, heart, stomach, or wherever you feel the most pain. It could be an enormous billowing, ominous cloud. Perhaps the cloud feels heavy, as if it is weighing on you or causing pressure. Or you may feel a strange, queasy sensation.

When you have concentrated on the sadness long enough to get the feeling of it, let go of the cloud. You could begin to let go by expelling it with your breath.

Let the sadness slowly billow out of your body like steam escaping from a teapot. Let it all escape. Feel the relief as you imagine it leaving. Then watch the dark cloud slowly but steadily float away, farther and farther away, drifting into the far-distant sky. Watch as it becomes smaller and smaller in the distance, like a bird flying away. Increasingly lose connection with it.

Finally, at the farthest horizon, the cloud totally disappears. Feel that you have lost any connection with the sadness. All the tension in your system has gone away, far away, and disappeared for good. Your body and mind feel light, relaxed, and free from even a trace of tension. Rest in that feeling.

Repeat this exercise a couple of times, as appropriate.

2. *Illuminating the Darkness of Sadness*

Visualizing light is another way to dispel sadness. If you feel that your mind is enveloped in confusion, depression, or hopelessness, with no vision of how to move or what to do, first imagine this sadness in the form of darkness. Visualize your whole body and mind as being filled with total darkness. Feel the sadness, without being overwhelmed by it. Then invoke healing light.

You could imagine the light as coming from your source of power. The light could come from within you, in front of you, or from above—wherever it feels right. See the beams of light— bright, warm, and joyful as a hundred suns—shining forth and touching you and instantly dispelling the darkness. Just as a beautiful flower blossoms with the touch of sunlight, your whole body and mind blossoms with joyful light.

The warm light fills your entire body, penetrating each and every cell, down to the atoms. You can imagine one of the cells as being an entire universe that is filled with light. The cell sparkles with light or shines with rays of colors. Or the healing light transforms the cell into some beautiful image or design of your own choosing.

Then imagine the light shining beyond your body, lighting the whole world. Feel the nature of the healing light—nonsubstantial, subtle, luminescent, pervasive, soft, limitless. Light is not solid, so there is nothing to grasp. Nothing can cause pressure or stress. Everything is light and immaterial.

Firmly believe that the darkness of sadness has totally disappeared for good, and a wonderful, health-giving light pervades the whole of existence. You, the world, and the light have become one. Rejoice and celebrate this. Taking short breaks, repeat this exercise again and again, finally relaxing in whatever you are feeling without the need of images.

You can extend this exercise into your daily life. When you turn on a light, or see the light of the sun or moon, see the light as pervading the darkness and bringing the power to heal.

### 3. Drying the Tears of Sorrow

If you feel habitually cold or chilled, the slightest mishap or negative mood can trigger a sensation that makes your whole body seem soaked in the tears of sadness.

Circulation problems, lack of exercise, and dietary or chemical imbalances can make us feel cold. So can problems at work or with our relationships, or even something as mundane as the weather. So we should recognize these causes and deal with them practically if possible.

However, we should also realize that our mind is the biggest cause of sadness, and such bodily expressions as cold are a reflection of our mind. It will help to develop an open, carefree attitude even in the face of problems, and to meditate in a way that brings warmth.

Calmly feel your sadness, and visualize it within your body as dark shadows or clouds soaked with wet tears. Above and in front of you, visualize your source of power as the center and essence of life-giving heat. You might imagine that the source is transformed into an orange sun-like ball of light and heat, or perhaps a deity.

Gradually visualize that bright rays from the image touch your head. See and feel the brightness and the heat. Feel that gradually the cold, the darkness, and the tears evaporate, as if a paper towel is being dried in the sun .

Do the same exercises stage by stage for every part of your body, from ears to toes. Then imagine that warmth, light, and a feeling of contentment fill your entire body, and then shine outside your body and warm your immediate surroundings, or even the entire universe. Meditate this way again and again. End with a feeling of openness.

### 4. *Clearing the Mirage of Fear*

When you are afraid, visualize your fears and doubts as a flickering shadowy mist or dark shadow in your body. Feel the mist. Then visualize a bright beam of powerful blessing light from your source of power touching the shadowy mist and totally expelling it from your body. Your whole body is filled with the strength of healing light. Rest within the warmth and strength.

You can also visualize in front of you a powerful divinity, either in peaceful or wrathful form, as you choose. In your mind's eye, look straight at him or her, and see and feel the amazing strength blazing forth from this divinity. Then pray to the divinity and ask for its strength, or imagine that the divinity changes into brilliant light and dissolves into yourself. Feel what it is like to be fearless now. Imagine that you are now able to move freely through the world or anywhere in the universe, without any lingering trace of fear. Repeat the exercise, resting within whatever empowering feelings of calm and space this meditation gives you.

### 5. Clearing the Underbrush of Worries

Even if we are happy and healthy, we might still harbor fear or anxiety in the depths of our minds and hearts. If we do not transform these emotions, they can forcefully manifest themselves when the opportunity arises.

If you spend some time quietly looking within, you may recognize some familiar worries or fears. In a friendly way, invite them to show themselves. Feel whatever bothersome emotions arise, and notice if they seem to come from a specific part of your body. Visualize an image that feels appropriate to your worries.

Perhaps the worries are like a dark light coming from a cave. Imagine that this strange dark light, which has been hidden or somehow "stuck" within you, now opens and shines forth effortlessly. All darkness leaves your body, vanishing completely.

You could also see your source of power as touching and dissolving the place where the darkness was hiding. Feel and believe that the habit of worrying has disappeared, and any worries that may have taken root out of sight are now gone for good. You could tell yourself, "I have no worries! It's wonderful to feel so free." Taste the delightful, lighthearted feeling of a mind and body free of worries.

### 6. Breaking the Self-Protective Shell of Sensitivity

If we let our habit of being emotionally sensitive grow because of our lack of self-confidence, eventually we'll experience most situations as a source of fear, danger, and pain. To heal our sensitive mental character, we need to break the habits of self-limitation, tightness, and vulnerability of our protective shell.

First, recognize and accept your sensitive feelings. Then, without dwelling on doubts and fears, imagine yourself as a subtle form—insubstantial, translucent, and open. You could think of yourself as composed of light, or immaterial like an image reflected in a mirror. Feel that you have nothing that needs to be protected. Nothing can hold or hurt you, and all harm passes right through you and is gone. As you contemplate this, believe that all feelings of vulnerability, sensitivity, and self-grasping have disappeared.

Without the need to worry so much about a solid, tight "self," you now can relax and enjoy your life. You can be fully present to whatever each moment brings, and react with confidence and warmth to the people you meet.

At the end of this exercise, you can call upon your source of power and feel that you are filled with healing light. The energy it can bring you reinforces mental strength and openness.

### 7. *Pacifying the Self-Criticizing Attitude*

Guilt is not always a bad thing. If we are arrogant, a healthy sense of guilt can diminish our egoism and prevent us from repeating mistakes. Yet many of us are overly self-critical. We grasp at guilt and lose the chance for fulfillment and enjoyment.

Do not feel guilty about your guilt—that only makes you feel more cold and rigid. Be glad for your guilt, for humility is positive. Any positive view can spontaneously become an inspiration and a healing, in the very moment we begin to shift our attitude. So see your self-criticism as a source of warmth. In your mind, surround it with a feeling of space and comfort.

Then let go of guilt as an unnecessary burden. Feel as if it weighs nothing at all, and allow it to drift away like a feather in a breeze.

Meditating on light, as described in other exercises, can help. Visualize your self-criticism or guilt as darkness, dark clouds, or mist. Imagine bright beams of light coming from your source of power, touching the guilt, warming it, making it feel insubstantial. The light fills your body, touching your heart and mind, dispelling all darkness. Without guilt, we can now feel joy, light, and warmth. Allow yourself to relax within any positive feelings that arise. Repeat this exercise again and again, and finally meditate in an open way.

### 8. Focusing Scattered Mind

When the mind is too sensitive and turned in on itself, we meditate to open up. On the other hand, for a mind that is aimless and uncontrollable, we need to develop concentration.

If your mind is wild and scattered like a leaf in the wind, practice one of the following exercises.

Imagine your body as huge and heavy like a mountain of gold, silver, or crystal. Visualize it as fixed and immovable on a vast golden plain. Feel the heavy, changeless, and unshakable nature of the body and its foundation. Let your own body and mind feel the heaviness. Repeat the exercise and rest in the feeling of heaviness.

Or visualize a statue of the Buddha as big as a golden mountain. Imagine its heaviness, solidity, power, and immovability. Repeat the exercise and rest in the sense of power and solidity.

Mindfulness in daily life also focuses and grounds us. For example, if you are reading, make a habit of concentrating on each word and its meaning, without thinking of something else. When you are not doing anything, concentration on your breathing is very effective.

### 9. Grounding Floating Energies

Another way to ground scattered energy is to imagine light that provides stability. When emotions and thoughts are unanchored, visualize healing light from your source of power descending through your entire body. From head to feet, feel the stabilizing power of this light. As it enters the soles of your feet, it brings you firmly down to earth. You are standing barefoot on a vibrant green field, ablaze with life and warmth. Concentrate on the feeling of your soles touching the rich, fertile earth. Feel that your restlessness is gone. Dwell within the pleasurable sensation of security and firmness as you stand in this beautiful place. Be at one with that feeling.

Here's a simple technique if you are bothered by floating feelings, wild thoughts, or anxieties. Focus your attention on the soles of your feet, which connect you to the earth. Also, gently massaging your soles in a relaxed and mindful way will call you back to your body and ground you.

### 10. Soothing Negative Memories

If you are upset by a stinging memory that persists, such as a negative incident at work, first see in your mind an image of the situation or the people involved, but without negative judgment or resistance. It can then help to visualize and feel that the memory is mist, clouds, smoke, or flame in your body. Purify the memory with an appropriate healing energy, such as light, wind, or soothing nectar. Linger for as long as you like in the feelings of comfort. Feel that the memory has been pacified, that you no longer need to suffer from its sting even if you remember the incident. Stay with that feeling of freedom as long as you can, rejoicing in it.

### 11. Cutting the Bonds of Unpleasant Relationships

If you feel that you are being emotionally bruised or frightened by a bad relationship or the memory of one, it is possible through meditation to cut your attachment to it. The exercises below can also release your bondage to excessively dependent relationships in which you feel too weak to stand on your own feet.

The problem or memory might be associated with someone at work, or perhaps a former romantic partner or spouse. Call up the negative feelings, and visualize that the other person is at some distance from you, dragging you forcefully around on a rope. You have no strength to stay still, and you are tossed about wildly.

Then pray, from the bottom of your heart, to your source of power for liberation. Visualize this source clearly, and imagine that it emits a sharp, laser-like blessing light aimed directly at the rope. By its touch the light not only breaks the rope, but burns it all up without leaving any trace, like paper consumed in a fire.

Or imagine being pulled and dragged about on a chain. As the blessing light touches the chain, it is pulled away from the hands of the person you are too dependent on, like iron being forcefully pulled away by a magnet. Then visualize the chain melting into soft, joyful light.

In either of these visualizations, enjoy the great relief of freedom from the harmful relationship. Feel your own inner strength. Relax in the positive feelings as long as you like.

If you must continue to see or work with the person who seems to be causing difficulties, the exercise can still be very effective. You can break free of the slavery to negative emotions, or at the very least become less bothered by them. If you are more cheerful and take the problem less seriously, the external situation can begin to improve.

## 12. *Relating to Others in the Light of Healing and Love*

We can be drawn into damaging emotions such as hatred or a craving for power over someone if we dwell on the feeling that that person is being cruel and unfair to us. Instead of nursing dislike and anger, try to see your enemy as intrinsically kind and good, even if you don't think he or she is really like that.

In Buddhism, the most kind and gentle human creature imaginable is thought of as a "mother-being." Imagine your enemy as a "mother-being" that has lost his or her way. This good person is blind with ignorance and sickness, victimized and tortured by his own emotional afflictions. He is endangering his own well-being by creating hellish worlds. If you can practice patience and compassion, your mind will become stronger and more steady. So this person is giving you a golden opportunity. He is like an employer who rewards you well for your work. To the extent he is cruel to you, and endangering his own spiritual well-being, you should be grateful to him for the chance to practice letting go of self and making true spiritual progress.

After generating these compassionate feelings, visualize that clouds of warm, white healing light emerge from your body and touch your enemy. By the mere touch of the light his body, heart, and mind are filled with happiness. He is amazed by feelings of peace and joy that he never thought possible. Allow him to celebrate and rest in that feeling. Then feel the warmth of compassion shining out to others, and even bathing the whole universe in warmth.

You could also visualize that light from your source of power touches your enemy and you, and you both melt into one body of light.

If you can meditate in this compassionate way, it will be easier to soothe your emotional pain and become more relaxed in the way you relate to others. When you are calm, you will be able to deal with real problems in a practical manner without being blindsided by negative emotions. The power of compassion will improve your relationship and generate the energy of peace and joy in both of you.

### 13. *Purifying Wrathful Dreams*

Bad dreams are a natural way of releasing mental energy, so we don't need to mind them—they could be interesting rather than frightening. However, if we are subject to intense nightmares that haunt and bother us, we can purify them by opening them up in meditation during our waking hours—or even while we are asleep, if we are skilled.

We should remind ourselves that any nightmare is a harmless creation of the mind. Also, healing light can pacify any disturbing image.

For example, if you keep dreaming you are trapped in a cell, touch the dream image with the healing light from the source of power, and see and feel the prison vanish.

Or, if something is repeatedly chasing you in your dreams,

when you finally feel ready to face it, you could stop and allow it to catch up. Be neither aggressive nor fearful, but touch it with healing light and transform it into peaceful and joyful images. It may change before your eyes into an image of peace!

### 14. Soothing Neurotic Symptoms

Some people are disturbed by illusions, omens, or feelings of a paranormal character, or by severe neurotic symptoms. Their waking hours are like a terrible nightmare.

Just as we are gentle with bad dreams that haunt our sleep, gentleness is appropriate for very disruptive neurotic disturbances.

For such disturbances, we should not be afraid to seek help and support from friends or wise counselors if it seems necessary. Healing meditations can also help to purify the underlying cause.

We should use our intellect to recognize that these disturbing experiences are false—mere mental fabrications or projections—even from the point of view of conventional truth. This in itself can ease our suffering.

We can also see such mental anguish as positive, since it points to the need to release and heal the underlying suffering. Neurotic symptoms result from the mind's grasping attempt to protect a deeper emotional or spiritual wound, just as our muscles painfully contract as a protective reflex around an injury or strain to the lower back. Our mental crisis gives us the chance to heal deeply. Eventually, we can be healthier and happier than before.

Be guided by the particular symptom and needs of the moment. If you can, use any of the exercises described so far, as appropriate to your symptoms. For example, if you feel trapped, meditating on light can help.

If you feel manic and out of control, rest quietly, and be mindful of the comfortable feeling of being in your body just as you are. Any meditation that calms or anchors us can help.

If you are extremely confused, calmly rest in the knowledge that confusion will pass with rest and healing. Even in this state of mind, you might find comfort in an inspirational picture or book. Gently bring your attention to one word at a time, even if that means only reading a sentence or paragraph.

If you feel paralyzed or weighted down by nervous symptoms, imagine those feelings in the form of an enormous weight. Then put it aside so that you can go take a walk or be with friends.

Sometimes it is best simply to be with your feelings in a relaxed way, to go along with the flow of emotions with the knowledge and belief that you can ride out the storm. Rest and be quiet. Always, adopt a caring attitude toward your own well-being.

*15. Extinguishing the Flame of Emotional Afflictions*

If you are experiencing a highly charged emotion such as craving, anger, or jealousy, take a step away from the emotion, calming yourself with a couple of long, relaxed breaths if necessary. Acknowledge the charge and fascination of the emotion, without being overwhelmed by it. Now visualize the emotion in your body as a blue flame. Feel the tingling sensation of this flame.

Then muster a strong conviction that you must guard your well-being. Invoke the force of the source of power. Imagine that a cool stream of healing nectar descends from the source of power, enters your body, fills it from head to toe, and extinguishes the destructive flame. Imagine any pleasant and healing sensation that helps you, such as coolness, or a deeply satisfying feeling of comfort and soothing. Feel and believe that the flame is gone. Be glad that at this very moment you are totally liberated from destructive emotion. Extend this spacious feeling for several minutes, or as long as you like. If possible, carry the calmness into an activity that will engage your attention and reinforce your healthy enjoyment and relaxation.

*16. Purifying Desires and Emotional Poisons*

Another meditation for strong afflictions, particularly if they feel earthy or solid, is to visualize them as dirt and impurities in the body. Feel that the emotion is like a poison that could make you sick if you cling to it. Firmly establish contact in your mind with the source of power, asking or praying to it for help. Then visualize that from the source of power a huge healing flame, symbolizing wisdom, comes toward you. Imagine it as a fierce but benevolent bonfire. By its mere touch, all the emotional dirt in your system is burnt to ashes. Then a stream of healing water, symbolizing compassion, flows into you, washing away all the ashes of your emotional dirt. Finally, strong, blessing air, symbolizing power, blows away all the impurities without leaving any trace behind. Experience being devoid of negative emotions.

Believe that the healing energies have released all your emotional tensions. Rest within the feeling of relief and liberation in your body and mind.

You can carry this meditative exercise into daily life by imagining that your afflictions are healed whenever you see or come in contact with any manifestation of fire, heat, water, or wind.

### 17. *Releasing Troubles with Your Breathing*

With all the many ways of healing, we can sometimes lose sight of a resource that is readily available to us—our breathing. The ability to visualize positive images is a very powerful tool. However, some people may want to release tension in another way, depending on their needs.

Perhaps you have grown tired of reading all the advice in this book, and require something easy! Here, then, is a very simple, effective exercise.

If you are under any kind of stress or emotional difficulty, bring awareness to your breathing, and especially to your exhalation. Allow your breathing in and out to become relaxed, while following your out-breath. Give yourself to your out-breath; relax into it. You may find that the out-breath becomes very relaxed and long, but whatever it is doing, simply allow your awareness to be with it. Stay with this for as long as you need to. This is a very simple healing that everyone can do.

## HEALING THROUGH SOUND

Visualization and the contemplation of breathing are two skillful means of healing. Another is the sound of our own voice.

Religions throughout history have used sound as a glorious expression of spirituality. So, too, in secular culture, music and singing seem to rise up spontaneously as a celebration of our humanity.

Certain sounds intrinsically make us feel open and relaxed. Singers familiar with music theory are aware of the joyful possibilities in using the "bright" vowels that are pronounced "ah," "ee," "ay" (as in *may*), "oh," and "oo." I am told that the songwriting of the traditional Broadway musical theater is built around allowing the singer to end a solo on a word that contains any of these sounds. The singer is able to hold the final note with a relaxed and open throat, the sound soars, and the resulting emotional release leaves everyone feeling happy.

We can bring healing sound into our meditation and daily life. Chanting is simple and accessible to all of us, but when done mindfully it can be a rich healing. Buddhist practice recommends certain words and sounds, although you may feel more comfortable choosing to chant or pray with sounds that are meaningful to you, such as any name of God according to your tradition, or a word like *amen, shalom* (Hebrew for "peace"), *peace*, or OM AH HUNG.

### *1. Soothing through the Sound of Openness*

In Buddhist scripture, AH is considered the source of all speech and sound—the source of openness. The gentle chanting of this sound is a soothing, openhearted meditation.

Allow the sound to come out naturally on your breath, pausing when you need to. Enjoy the sound of your voice, and imagine that the whole world is filled with peaceful sound. Then imagine that the all-pervading sound conveys the following message to you, in a strong but nurturing voice: "All feelings of imperfection, all guilt, all negative energies in you are completely purified! Now you are pure, healthy, and perfect! Celebrate and rejoice!" Feel that the sound instantly evokes a strong feeling of warmth and healing, and relax in that experience. Then merge with your chanting for a while. Simply be at one with the sound.

You can also heal injuries caused by negative words. If you feel guilt or resentment toward anyone—your father, for example—imagine that within the positive sound you hear his voice saying again and again, with kindness and honesty, some words such as this: "I am thankful and happy to have you as a son or daughter. We both have shortcomings, but who doesn't? We should forgive each other. Child, be yourself, whatever you are. I love you." Calmly experience the meaning and feeling of these words. Then, through the sound of your chanting, you can tell him: "Thank you for telling me what you feel! I am very happy that you are my father! I love you, Father!" Then feel that all your relationship problems with your father have disappeared like mist in the summer sun, and that you feel calm and at peace.

Relationships don't always change overnight, but such a meditation can purify the resentments within us if we practice it wholeheartedly. This could eventually lead to dramatic improvement.

Another use of sound involves encouraging ourselves out loud. When problems come, try telling yourself that everything is perfectly fine, even in its imperfections. Choose the words that fit your personality and needs. The potency of sound can magnify the positive effect of ordinary words or prayers.

Some of us are reluctant to make any sound at all. For overly sensitive people, sound can be just the thing to release such feelings as fear and doubt. If you are shy about others hearing you, find a secluded place. When I was growing up in Tibet, young monks would practice their chanting by the banks of roaring rivers. In a city, you could chant or sing near a busy, noisy street where no one will notice or care. Warm up slowly and with your relaxed out-breath build to a loud AH or any sound that feels natural. Really let go—it's your right to make a joyful noise!

## 2. Healing through Blessed Sound

The sounds OM, AH, and HUNG (pronounced *hoong*, with a soft *h*) are viewed as the "seed syllables" of the body, speech, and mind of the Buddha, the fully enlightened nature. Because of the universality of these sounds, anyone can benefit from them.

These three syllables comprise one of the most powerful chants in Buddhism. They are pure and archetypal in nature, free from elaboration, concepts, grasping, and rigidity. So just giving voice to these sounds allows us to be more open.

For Buddhists, these sounds also embody special meaning in their expression of all the qualities of the Buddha: OM is the changeless strength and beauty of the true nature we all possess, the Buddha body; AH is the ceaseless expression and prevailing energy of reality, the Buddha speech; HUNG is the unmoving perfection of reality's primordial openness, the Buddha mind. Long used in healing practices, these sounds have been blessed by many Buddhas and enlightened beings throughout the ages.

Each syllable represents particular healing qualities. Singing OM brings peace, bliss, clarity, firmness, courage, stability, and strength; AH brings energy, openness, expansion, and empowerment; HUNG is associated with enlightenment, infinity, essence, and oneness.

You can sing each syllable with equal emphasis. Or else emphasize and repeat one syllable according to the particular healing qualities you need. For example:

```
OOOOOOOOOOMMMM AHHHHHHHHHHHH HUUUUUUUUNNNNNGGG
OOOOOOOOOOOOOOOOOOOMMMMMMM AHHHHH HUUUUNNNGGG
OOOOMM AHHHHHHHHHHHHHHHHHHHHHHHHHHH HUUUNNNGGG
OOOOMM AHHHHHHHHHH HUUUUUUUUUUUUUUUUUUUUNNNNNGGG
```

Sing the syllables however you feel is soothing—in a tune that rises and falls or on one note, quietly or loudly, with high pitch or low, with soft or thundering sound.

You can work with these sounds to transform difficult thoughts, feelings, and images. Feel as if sadness or painful emotion is contained within the sound of OM in the form of clouds, smoke, or mist. As you sing AH, let go of the problems forever. With HUNG, feel the healing of peace and openness.

You can also call forth your source of power with these syllables (or with the sound of AH alone). Feel that the sound is invoking and generating all the healing forces of the universe, and that the source of power emerges from and is itself an embodiment of the sound. See and feel warm, bright light radiating from the sound and the image. The light gradually fills your head and entire body. As you continue chanting, take your time celebrating the sound and the light, which brings healing to every part of mind and body.

### 3. *Purifying Our Emotions Silently*

Chanting can be silent too. An exercise called "threefold breathing" involves saying the three seed syllables to ourselves in unison with our breathing. This develops concentration and strength of mind, purifies negative emotions, and can be a good preliminary to any other healing meditation.

In threefold breathing, mentally say OM as you inhale. Say AH as you pause, in the moment when the breath is about to begin moving the other way. Say HUNG on the out-breath. Feel that you are breathing in unison with the body, speech, and mind of the Buddha, and all Buddhas of all time. If you are more comfortable with a secular approach, appreciate these syllables as the universal embodiment of strength, openness, and oneness.

Let your breath and the syllables flow naturally. Give yourself fully to this, so that your breathing, the syllables, and your mind become one. Finally, allow your silent chanting to dissolve into relaxed breathing, let go of the syllables, and merge within the silence of your breathing.

Amid the din of modern life, it is tempting to fall back on noisy distractions that take us away from our true selves. Perhaps we are afraid of silence, like children afraid of the dark. By giving ourselves wholly to chanting or singing, produced by the body in union with the mind, we learn to appreciate sound. Then it becomes easier to fully appreciate silence.

# 9

# HEALING PHYSICAL DISHARMONY ~

BUDDHISTS BELIEVE that disharmony between mind and body is at the root of sickness. Healing through meditation creates harmony, emotional and physical, which helps release potentially harmful blocks and vitalizes the body even down to the level of cells.

According to ancient Tibetan medicine, the body is a composite of the elements of water, fire, air, and earth, as well as heat and cold. Modern science has given us an intricate and wonderful picture of the body, but even today the traditional map passed down to us from ancient Buddhist scripture still works as an aid in harnessing our inner resources.

We would have to go deeply into the study of medical traditions of the East to understand all the rich insights into emotion, body, and mind. However, for our purposes, the heart of the matter is positive attitude. Although it can help to determine whether an ailment is hot or cold, Westerners generally have limited experience in this approach.

Virtually any meditative approach that makes us feel comfortable and good can help us both emotionally and physically.

The exercise on awakening the healing energy in our cells, described in chapter 7, could be particularly relevant to physical problems. We could use any exercise aimed at clearing energy blocks. Or, at any time, we could draw refreshment and comfort simply by meditating on our source of power.

If you feel that a particular emotional problem may be at the root of your physical symptoms, you could meditate to release it. But it isn't necessary to pinpoint or concentrate upon a particular mental obstruction that needs healing. The simple intention to let go of emotional blocks is beneficial in itself.

A relaxed and open meditation aimed at one specific problem can dissolve other problems and lift our spirits. Meditation can be a powerful physical healer. Even when we can't banish a physical ailment, meditation can help free our minds, which is the most important healing of all.

## LIGHT THAT HEALS PHYSICAL AILMENTS

In Tibetan Buddhism, visualizations of light are the most popular means of healing both emotional blocks and physical complaints.

Create a relaxed atmosphere for yourself before beginning any visualization, whether for relief from a mental block or for such physical ailments as a tumor or artery blockages. Take a deep breath or follow your calm breathing for a while.

If the blockage is cold or you feel it as cold, for just a little while feel it as icy, hard, or chilled. Then imagine your source of power in front of you and a little above. Allow a comforting and expansive feeling of belief in the healing power of your mind to rise up within you. Now call forth a flame-like light from your source of power. If your source of power is a visualized divinity, the flaming light could flow from the eyes, hand, or body of the divinity.

The warm red light penetrates the blockage. If it is a cold blockage in your head, feel warmth and comfort there at the touch of the light. Imagine the icy block slowly melting, dissolving completely into water. The water slowly runs down through the body, through your throat, chest, stomach, and legs, and out from your soles, toes, and lower doors, totally disappearing into the ground.

You may also work with warm or cool blockages as follows. If your sickness is related to heat, visualize a cool white light coming from the source of power and encircling the upper part of your body. It attracts all your sickness, like magnetized metal, and exits from the top of your head and dissolves into the sky. If your sickness feels cold, visualize a warm red light from the source of power encircling your abdomen and the lower part of your body. It attracts the sickness and exits from your feet, dissolving into the earth.

If the pain or obstruction feels sharp like a stone, stick, nail, or knife, first visualize it in such a form. Then imagine that by the mere touch of the light from the source of power, the nail-like pain is instantly extracted from the body, like the sudden extraction of a splinter or a thorn. Believe that it has been completely pulled out and is gone, with no trace of pain. Rest in the feeling of peace, relief, and the energy of good health.

If you have a tumor, after briefly focusing on its location and approximate form, you could visualize a very bright, sharp, laser-like light coming from your source of power. The mere touch of the light cuts the growth into minuscule pieces, and they disintegrate into their component atoms. These atoms are pushed down through your body and dissolve into the ground, or exit when you next urinate or defecate.

If you have arteries clogged with plaque, first sense them and their location. Then use powerful healing light from the source of power to dilute, melt, purify, and clear all the harmful deposits. Feel again and again that your arteries are opened wide and clear, with blood and energies coursing through them without a trace of obstruction.

And so, depending on the need, we can visualize healing

light in a variety of forms—as hot light, warm light, sharp light, or cool light. Some people also imagine broom-like rays of light that sweep away sickness, or sprinkles of light like water that wash away the impurities of the body.

Use the method that feels best to you. For example, if your nerves or muscles are being pressured or crushed, do the appropriate conventional physical exercises or therapy with the feeling that warmth-giving light is helping to open up your joints, releasing pressures, and healing any damaged tissue.

## WATER THAT HEALS PHYSICAL AILMENTS

Like light, water is often recommended as an image in meditation to awaken inner healing and purification.

Imagine water as a nectar-like medicinal stream. From your source of power it descends through your head and flows through your body, soothing and cleansing every part of it, and in particular restoring the flow and harmony among the cells affected by sickness. Feel and believe that it is washing away dirt and detoxifying poisons. Your body becomes pure like a clean, clear bottle.

Repeat the exercise again and again; then see the stream filling your body. You could imagine it filling even your tissue and blood cells, bringing purity and health. Finally, relax within your feelings.

You could imagine the medicinal stream as hot, diluting and melting down cold mental or physical blocks, such as tumors, like hot water being poured on ice. Or, if the blockage seems hot, as in a burning or stinging sensation, imagine a cool stream of nectar or water that slowly extinguishes the flame. Feel the coolness as it flows through you. Finally, the flame is out, and the stream slowly runs through your body, washing away the ashes of sickness, and all blockage, through your lower doors, soles, and toes into the ground. Feel the peace and coolness.

## FIRE, AIR, AND EARTH FOR HEALING

Although not as prominent in traditional healing as light and water, the elements of fire, air, and earth could be very effective, depending on your own feelings and needs.

*Fire:* Waves of healing flame come to you, enveloping every cell of your body. The flame radiates warmth, health, and happiness. It burns and consumes all physical ailments related to coldness, lifelessness, or lack of energy.

*Air:* Pure air sweeps away such ailments as circulatory and respiratory weakness, or congestions and toxins in the cells of your body. The blessed air purifies and amplifies the healthy qualities of your breathing and circulation, bringing health to every cell of your body. You could imagine that this wind is like beautiful music within you. If you have a radio or tape player by your sickbed, you could hear the actual sound of music as if it were within your body, granting relaxation and health.

*Earth:* When sickness brings doubts, fears, or panic, we can remind ourselves not only of the intrinsic strength of our mind, but also of how resilient our body is. Feel your body as solid and strong, and take some time to rejoice in its fundamentally earth-like qualities. Visualize your whole body as being like the earth, unshakable and self-renewing, despite the passing weaknesses or tremors of sickness. Bring as much detail to the exercise as you like. See your body's bones, muscles, nerves, skin, and chemicals as strong. Imagine the earth within you, that your body or cells are solid as mountains, healthy and regenerative as trees, beautiful as all of nature.

## HEALING WITH THE HELP OF OTHERS

In Tibet, spiritual masters traditionally serve others by overseeing the welfare of both mind and body. As dispensers of physical healing, accomplished masters rely on the esoteric teachings of tantric Buddhism, including meditation, mantra recitation, and such materials as blessed medicinal herbs and plants.

For the most advanced practices of esoteric Buddhism, you would need strong meditative experience, a familiarity with the tantric sources, and direct transmission from an authentic master. However, the ordinary teachings in the scriptures make it clear that anyone can benefit from healing through rituals performed by other people.

Westerners who pride themselves on their rationalism may reject the idea of healing through the channel of a healer. They may say, "Oh, this is a lot of mumbo jumbo," or "I don't believe in magic." And yet people who think of themselves as quite modern and rational often put great faith in medical doctors. This secular "faith" is related to the modern treatment, but also goes beyond it—a good doctor can help to instill positive attitude. This is very empowering, since it can galvanize a patient's inner resources and assist the immune system in benefiting from conventional treatment.

We heal ourselves, but others can help us to heal. This is the Buddhist view, and it is also common sense. So it makes sense in choosing a conventional doctor to seek someone with a good "bedside manner," a partner who can assist us in our own healing with a spirit of rapport and openness.

Common sense also tells us that we should be glad for the healing love that others can give us. People who feel they are loved are better able to deal with sickness. Love nourishes our mind, like a flower in sunshine. The sharing of emotions offered by support groups can be helpful. Even if we are alone in our sickness, we can love ourselves in an open, relaxed way. This is proper and powerful.

It's also possible to receive healing from others through meditation. While many of us may feel most comfortable using the healing exercises by ourselves, some can benefit from another person who acts as healer.

The following method, adapted from Tibetan Buddhist

sources, can be very empowering if we are open to it. Healing energy already lies within us, but sometimes we need help outside ourselves to unlock it.

For this exercise, you and the healer need to be well disposed toward each other, and to share an openness to meditation. Lie down with your eyes closed. Both you and the healer should take a couple of deep breaths, feeling that all the negative energies of the body and mind are expelled with the exhalation. Then relax in the feeling of calm and spaciousness for a while, before silently visualizing the exercise together.

For general healing purposes, healing light comes through the healer's hands from the source of power. Alternatively both you and the healer could visualize him or her as the source of power.

The healer holds his or her hands flat and open, palms down just slightly above the midsection of your body or at the point of the pain or negative energies. Visualize that healing light is drawing away all sickness, sadness, and worry. Barely touching your body, the healer's hands slowly move to your shoulders and down your arms. You both should firmly believe that all sickness is swept away, as the healer makes a throw-away gesture with his or her hands that sweeps illness out through your fingertips.

The healer then slowly performs this again from the point of sickness, but this time in the other direction, taking your sickness out through your feet. Repeat the purification again as many times as you feel the need and are comfortable.

Another approach is to have the healer gently massage the affected area with his or her palm(s) in a slow, clockwise motion. Both the healer and receiver should visualize and feel that a shower of light full of healing energies—heat, bliss, and joy—is being channeled from the source of power through his or her hand(s), like sun rays streaming through a window. Imagine the hands as a window to the source of power, which directly transmits warm, bright, health-giving light. Because of the healer's warm and generous feelings toward you, the healing power is magnified as if through a magnifying glass or prism that channels light.

All the ill effects are cleansed, and like flowers blooming with the touch of sunlight, the cells blossom with healing energies. When you feel that the cells are open with healing energy and your body is saturated with it, the healer should hold his or her hand(s) still to stabilize the energy. Both of you can bask in the energies of good health that are generated, finally resting in openness.

Similar exercises could use images of laser-like light that turns illness into ashes that are swept away, or streams of nectar that wash away sickness and fill the body's weak places with health.

Some people may benefit from prayers offered by others, or the power of sacred objects or places. If a spiritual practice is offered for you, try to establish some physical link with the source. Making a financial contribution, if it is a token of true generosity, can help you feel more open. In all cases, faith in the source of healing is essential.

When I was about fifteen, many people worked for a month or so to rebuild my house at the monastery. Two women helping with the construction were very sick. Medicine wasn't helping them. They had *peken trethog*, a phlegm-humor disorder that was one of the biggest health problems in our area, especially for the elderly. The disease prevents people from swallowing or digesting food and slowly starves them to death. I used to make a dough of *tsampa*, roasted barley flour and butter, and after blessing it with prayers, give it to them. They had no problem eating it.

Before leaving they took a large quantity of the blessed *tsampa* dough to mix, a little at a time, with their meals. After many months, they were completely cured. This disease afflicted many, both monks and laymen, including my own grandfather, who died from it when I was about four, and my grandmother, who survived thanks to either the blessed *tsampa* that I gave her or medicine that she took her entire life, as far back as I can remember. She did not succumb to starvation, but was never cured either.

To make the blessed *tsampa* dough, I visualized Guru Rinpoche above in the sky in front of me as I kneaded the flour and butter. Repeating the prayer-mantra, I opened myself with strong devotion from the depth of my heart and invoked his healing blessings. I visualized that from Guru Rinpoche healing energies in the form of amazing warm and blissful lights, or sometimes in the form of streams of nectar, came down and merged into the dough. Then, with conviction, I thought that the dough was empowered with blessings to heal the phlegm disorder.

The dough could heal because of the three principles of healing. The ladies had full trust in my healing power. They were karmically open to receive the blessing. And my devotion was strong enough to invoke the healing power.

## HEALING AWARENESS OF PHYSICAL AND ENERGY MOVEMENTS

Lie down on your back on a comfortable mattress, using pillows for support to relax the muscles of your body. Then slowly and calmly go through the following exercises, taking a minute or two for each step.

1. Taking one or two deep breaths, let go of all your stress and worries with your outgoing breath and relax the body and mind.

2. Be aware of and feel your whole body. Feel the calmness that pervades your whole body as the result of relaxing.

3. Be aware of your back resting on the mattress, and feel how gravity gently pulls you toward the earth. This will help settle your floating energies and flickering thoughts.

4. With a sense of boundlessness, be aware of your breathing: not only the air in your lungs, but the breathing in every cell in your body, from the crown of your head to the soles of your

feet. As the cells breathe, they move up and down in a natural, calm, open, and steady motion.

5. Feel the movement and energy in every part of your body: arteries, veins, nerves, muscles, blood, organs, brain, spine, bones, and skin—especially in the part that needs to be healed.

Then, with awareness of that calm energy, enjoy the following exercise for about ten to twenty minutes:

Very slowly and naturally move the part that you need to heal backward and forward, up and down, or to the side. You could take a minute or two to move it toward one side, and then a minute or two to move it toward the other side. During this movement, it is important to be calmly, one-pointedly, and completely aware of the stream of movement. Be aware of how even the tiniest movement in this one part of your body is felt throughout the rest of your body, like a chain of waves. Be aware of the intimate calm and bliss circulating within you through the movements.

Sometimes you do not even need to initiate any physical movement. You can just imagine the movement, or imagine your energy moving with the awareness of the feelings.

After this exercise, you could add the following exercise for a few minutes:

Imagine and feel that a shower of blessing lights (or a stream of blessing nectar) pours from the source of power into your body so that your body is filled with it, especially the part that needs to be healed. Feel that the energy of heat and bliss from the blessing light (or nectar) is magnified, like oil on a flame, and be aware of the waves of blissful heat that this generates in your body.

Conclude this exercise by relaxing in the state of awareness of the body and mind in oneness and openness, without grasping or discriminations.

This exercise grounds your floating mind and energies. It unites your body and mind in harmony. It cultivates positive perceptions and healthy energies. And it awakens the awareness of strength, peace, and joy, the healing qualities of your mind and body.

After becoming skilled in this exercise, you could try to use the same awareness of healing energy in your other daily activities, such as thinking, feeling, walking, looking, standing, sitting, sleeping, speaking, and working.

# 10

# HEALING WITH NATURE'S ENERGY ～

THE TRUE SOURCE and the final goal of spiritual awakening is in the mind, not in nature. Nevertheless, nature can be a great comfort to us. An appreciation of nature gives us an immediate and direct opportunity to get out of ourselves and our concerns. It takes so little effort for any of us to open to nature. Merely by opening our eyes and senses, the sheer beauty of the natural world can bring us closer to our true selves. When awareness opens, we are being led to the true nature of our mind.

I became aware of the soothing power of nature at a very young age in Tibet. The wind through the trees and valleys was like music, the rivers had their own song. Even the total silence seemed like a kind of music. We can all draw sustenance and warmth from the majestic, fatherly power of mountains, the generous lights of sun and moon, or the vast presence of the ocean. Even if we live in a crowded city or suburb, nature is present in a leaf on a sidewalk or the wetness of a hedge after rainfall. Wherever we are, above all is the ever-tolerant motherly openness of the sky and space.

Of course we don't need to compare nature to anything at

all. Nature can soothe and warm us, but ultimately it is beyond metaphors and concepts. We use words to describe it, but the purest experience of nature is to simply be aware of it as it is. Nature is free from limits, labels, pressures, or stresses. By enjoying nature in an open way, with unadorned awareness, we can soften the walls of our mental discriminations and graspings.

Sometimes we might feel lonely or desolate in the middle of nature's vastness. This is only our small "self" being reminded of itself. Rather than worrying about this, we can be gentle with our feelings. We can actually be gladdened by this desolation. If we are relaxed within our loneliness, this can be an awakening. In many ways, nature can help us release the tightness of self.

According to Buddhism, the physical world, including our bodies, is made of the elements earth, water, fire, air, and space. Contemplating the positive qualities of these elements in nature, whether in the form of a tree, a flower, or the ocean, is a natural kind of healing.

## EARTH

Mother Earth majestically tolerates everything, good or bad, strong or weak. Earth is present for all during prosperity and barrenness alike. Earth is peaceful whether the sun shines or a storm rages, unchanging by day or night. It is our solid foundation—our home.

With care and respect, sit or lie stretched on your back on the bare earth, sand, or rock. Touch it with your hands or feet. Feel its solidity, strength, and majestic nature. By contemplating and feeling its strong, stable nature, your mind spontaneously takes on those very qualities.

Imagine that all the unhealthy energies in your body that cause you worry, insecurity, and unproductiveness are eliminated. Become one with the earth's boundless strength. Be thankful for this healing energy, for the tolerance and bounty of the earth that sustains us.

Focusing on the intrinsic character of earth as strong and solid is beneficial for people who have speedy, dreamy, floating, or weak minds, or who lack common sense, concentration, discipline, or solid direction.

## WATER

Contemplate the calm, cool, cleansing, synthesizing, harmonizing nature of water. Enjoy the flow of a river, which is simultaneously consistent, strong, and forever harmonizing and synthesizing. At the ocean, enjoy the vastness; let your senses be saturated with the bracing air and the sound and sight of the unceasing waves. Watch the play of the waves, feel the energy, the beauty of the rising, cresting, and falling.

In drinking water, fully experience the satisfaction of quenching your thirst. In touching water, feel its purity. In bathing or swimming, feel its soothing nature. Let yourself feel as though all your problems are being purified and cleaned. When it rains, feel the soothing nature of rain. Feel as though the rain is nourishing life and growth within you.

By sitting quietly by a calm lake or a flowing stream, your mind quite naturally settles into calmness and clarity. Water in its purity promotes a sense of reverence in us. If you can't be near a body of water that inspires you, visualizing that you are sitting by such a scene can bring peaceful feelings to your mind.

For people who have trouble being consistent, unifying their lives, or bringing plans to fruition, it can help to contemplate the consistent, calm, flowing energy of water—its intrinsic character of nourishing life and holding things together.

## FIRE

Fire destroys, but it also generates. Warmth and light allow life to grow, blossom, ripen, and mature.

In meditation, focus on the forceful, powerful, blazing character of fire. In everyday life, be glad for the sun's warmth, light, and pervasive energy. Imagine that all the negative or dead energies and problems in your life are transformed or burned away by healing fire. Feel that your mind and body are filled with warmth and blazing energy that ripen your own positive qualities. Feel the warmth and be at one with it. Imagine the whole universe filled with infinite energy of fire, and rejoice in its healing power.

Contemplating the intrinsic warmth and heat of fire is especially beneficial for people who lack inspiration and motivation to fulfill their goals and engage fully in life.

## AIR

Air gently envelops us, granting life and breath. Be aware of air in all its manifestations, in its stillness and in its moving, changeable qualities. Welcome the force of the powerful wind, as if it is carrying you through the sky. Welcome the breeze's gentle caress on your face and body, as if it is lovingly touching every cell and organ. Concentrate on your breathing and be aware of its every movement, as if the universe and you have become one in the peaceful continuum of breathing.

See and feel the amazing nature of air, utterly light and all-pervasive. Imagine that by the touch of healing air all negative energies and problems are lifted or blown away from your body and mind without a trace. Imagine yourself filled with the all-pervading energy and lightness of air.

Feeling the intrinsic lightness and movement of air—in everyday life or in visualization exercises—can inspire people who feel slow, heavy, dull, lazy, and uninspired. However, anyone with an excitable, fast mind needs to be skillful and balanced in using the healing energy of air.

By contemplating the openness of space, the only nonphysical element, we can experience the openness of our own nature.

Space is emptiness and immateriality. Space provides the room for everything else, including the other physical elements.

Look out at the deep blue sky and feel its immaterial, non-grasping nature. See and feel its vastness and limitless quality—the infinity of sky. Be aware, in your mortal body, of space and openness beyond questions or elaborations, beyond time or place. Let go of your thoughts and worries, and be at one with the nature of sky. We can feel great peace looking at the sky, especially from a place with a broad view on a clear day. But any glimpse of the sky can grant us peace. Gazing at the night sky, especially when it is clear, will also encourage a meditative state of mind.

The boundless sky has more than enough room for our suffering. Practice releasing into space all your pain, stresses, and grasping. Imagine that all worries and negative thoughts disappear there, like mist or clouds that disperse without a trace. Appreciate any feeling of comfort or peace that comes to you.

## TREES

Trees can be a great source of healing for the mind. The Buddha experienced the total openness of enlightenment while sitting beneath the shelter of a tree.

Contemplating the beauty of trees is a simple way to connect ourselves with the healing energy of nature. First, consider the qualities of a tree: its amazing character, which to our eyes is changeless and ageless day in and day out; its strength in wind, storm, or sun; its tolerance of cold or heat; its beauty in snow or rain; its aliveness.

Contemplate with your full attention the mass of green

leaves, which may be ornamented with blossoms, flowers, fruits, seeds, or nuts. You can also look closely at one single leaf or nut, and appreciate its amazing beauty and vitality in miniature.

The roots of a tree are anchored in the ground. Appreciate the mountain-like strength and stability of the tree. Appreciate, too, the flexibility of a tree. Its branches move and sway gracefully in the wind in the day or night, as if in a dance of celebration beyond any concept or name. Open your awareness to how strong, beautiful, and magnificent a tree is. This allows feelings of warmth and strength to spontaneously grow within you.

You may also draw healing energy from a tree by sitting still under or near it, or by wrapping your arms around its trunk. The tree is connected to the power of the earth through its roots, and to the forces of the cosmos above through its leaves and branches. The trunk is a living bridge between the solar forces above and the earth below. The branches, which extend outward, represent the tree's giving and receiving nature.

Silently ask the tree to allow you to experience the energy of its nature. Then, as you gently touch the trunk, feel that you are connecting within this natural energy, and feel your own positive energy rising within you. Recognize any healing energy that you experience, and be glad for whatever positive feelings you have. Rest within these feelings, letting all ideas and thoughts dissolve into the energy of the moment. In return, give the tree your appreciation and love.

You can draw healing energies from all of nature's creations based on the principles in this exercise. In our relaxed contemplation of our world, we should develop an appreciation for all of nature in its power and limitlessness, without trying to grasp or capture it.

# 11

# DAILY LIVING AS HEALING ~~

ONE OF THE most important and effective means of healing is to turn every step of our daily life into healing exercises. Instead of separating meditation and life into compartments, bring them together. By bringing a spacious awareness into whatever you do, equanimity, clarity, and joy have a chance to blossom. If we develop the right habits, everything becomes a healing. So we should consistently try to develop a right way of seeing, thinking, and acting.

Mindfulness is the key to transforming our daily lives. Let go of worries and habitual dislikes, and simply be with the stream of your activities. Cultivate a relaxed and open mood, whether you are thinking with your intellect or acting with your body. When you are walking, standing, sitting, or lying down, give yourself to that. When you are looking at a table or a painting, or listening to music or a person, give yourself to the looking or listening. Be wholly with whatever you are doing. This brings openness and awareness and loosens the tightness of self.

Approach your life in the spirit of warm-hearted enjoyment. Only a few dates on the calendar are marked as holidays, but we don't have to wait for them to be cheerful and happy. Even when problems or challenges come, an open attitude will guide us along the path.

Tibetan Buddhist scriptures offer many specific techniques

for turning daily activity into spiritual practice. As always, we need to know what advice best fits our needs.

Yukhog Chatralwa, a great master whom I knew in my early teens, gave an instruction that unifies all of life within the practice of contemplating a divinity, which for us could be any source of power:

> While sitting, visualize the peerless and gracious precious
> master [the source of power]
> On the crown of your own head and
> Again and again receive the blessing [lights].
> This unites your own mind with the realized mind of the
> master.
> While you are doing daily activities, see that all the appearing
> forms are the forms of the master,
> All sounds are the melodies of his speech, and
> All your good and bad thoughts are his wisdom mind.
> This is the instruction on phenomenal existents arising as the
> virtues of the master.
> While eating, visualize the master in your throat and
> Offer him the nectar of food and drink.
> Then food and drink will create no defilements in you, and
> It will be turned into a sacramental celebration.
> While sleeping, visualize him in the center of your heart.
> The lights of his body illuminate the world and all beings.
> Transform them into light and then dissolve them into
> yourself.
> This is the instruction on turning sleep and dreams into
> luminous absorption.
> When you are leaving for the next existence [death],
> Without shuffling in too many worries,
> Contemplate on the unification of your own awareness, and
> The enlightened mind of the master.

## AWAKENING

Waking up can be a time of great warmth and peace. The body and mind live together naturally in sleep, and then comes the dawn of our awareness in the morning. Instead of jumping into the turmoil of the day's obligations, take your time experiencing the union of body and mind. Be at ease with the relaxed and open feeling.

Take a relaxed, deep breath or two, and release any tensions or impurities that may have accumulated overnight. Allow a few minutes to be with your body and feelings. Enjoy the natural warmth of the body, from your head to the soles of your feet. Simply be open, in a limitless way. Sense the feeling of warmth and openness and be one with it.

This mind and body orientation could be the basis in a very simple way for the rest of your day. As you are getting up to begin your morning, you can think, "I will be mindful of using this awakening and energy as the basis of the day's activities." Then, during the day, from time to time, bring back the warmth and calmness you felt upon awakening, and let it permeate your mind like the calmness and energy of the vast ocean beneath its waves.

Even if you feel an emotional ache of some kind upon awakening, the dawn of awareness presents a good moment for healing. Because awareness is so open as we awake, we can merge our consciousness with the ache, and the feeling may then become more peaceful. If you feel anxiety as you begin the day, gently ease yourself into your activities, and the mood can change. Or you could use a healing exercise to clear the blocked energy.

When you wake up, you can also imagine you are waking from the ignorance of sleep and opening your mind's eye to the wisdom of peace, joy, light, and awareness. You can wish the same for all beings.

It is difficult not to think, the very instant we wake, about our usual, immediate mundane worries, desires, and emotions. However, if we return to the spacious feeling, instead of clinging to these emotions or following our mind as it rushes off like the wind, we will gradually develop the habit of waking with this attitude spontaneously.

Various Buddhist trainings encourage this attitude. One is

to imagine you are awakened in the morning from the sleep of ignorance by the joyous voices of enlightened beings—what Buddhists call "wisdom divinities"—or the sounds of their musical instruments, such as hand drums. Another is to receive blessings from your source of power.

## RECEIVING BLESSINGS

Before falling asleep at night, visualize the source of power in your heart or above you, radiating blessing lights during your sleep. Immediately upon waking, feel the presence of the source of power already above you. Or visualize it ascending through your body and then sitting above the crown of your head, as guide and protector. Enjoy the warmth and strength of this presence. Share your feelings with the whole universe, and take peace and joy with you into the day.

## WASHING AND CLEANING

When washing your face, teeth, or body, imagine that all the impurities—of sicknesses, emotional afflictions, and tensions—are washed away by pure water and that your whole being shines with healing energy.

When you feel tense, you can use chores as a healing, just as in the story of the Buddhist patriarch Lamchungpa that is related in chapter 4. When you are cleaning your room, washing your clothes, or taking out your garbage, imagine that your emotional, mental, or physical impurities are also being cleaned or taken away like the dust and garbage.

## BREATHING

Breathing is the thread on which life hangs. It is the intimate life force upon which every being constantly depends. If we can turn breathing into the support of our spiritual healing, our training will pervade every part of our life.

Take a few slow, deep breaths with the intention of releasing worries or negativities. When you feel tight or under stress, allow your breathing to be completely relaxed. Be glad of any positive feeling, even the smallest shift in mood or sense of openness. Wish that all beings could experience peace and release from suffering.

Awareness of breathing from time to time throughout the day brings us home to ourselves. During physical exercise, you can magnify the mental and physical benefits by breathing freely in conjunction with your body's movements and enjoying the sense of release and energy of the breath.

## DRINKING AND EATING

In the early morning, it is healthful to drink a cup of hot water. It purifies the digestive system, dilates the tissues, and improves the circulation of the blood and energy. It is important to enjoy good, healthy food and drink in moderate quantity. Food should be consumed not in a vain attempt to fill emotional desires but in accord with your actual physical needs. See the food you eat as sustaining and nourishing, and enjoy it by being mindful of every taste you take. Try to be aware of the process of each sip of liquid and bite of food, and consciously follow the food's movements in your body as far as you can. Feel that the food and drink are not only satisfying your hunger and thirst, but also generating health in body and mind. Wish the same enjoyment for all beings. Appreciate and be thankful for the pleasure of every sip and bite you take.

A number of Buddhist trainings treat food as the means of healing. For example, imagine that blessing lights from the source of power transform the food into healing nectar. Then enjoy it as a blessed substance that grants you joy and strength.

Or, as you enjoy the food, think: "This food is giving me strength to enhance my own life and serve others."

Or think of the food as a pure and wonderful gift, and offer it to the source of power. Visualize the source of power accepting the offering with pleasure and blessing it for your benefit in return. Then enjoy the food with awareness that it is blessed. This training combines devotion with practices of generosity and pure perception.

Or, with compassion for the innumerable beings who live in your body in the form of bacteria, enjoy the food, knowing that it will sustain them too.

Or, with pure perception, visualize yourself in the form of a deity, or even as an assembly of hundreds of deities. Enjoy the food as a blessed offering, a skillful means of wisdom, that brings the realization of peace and bliss.

## WALKING

Taking a walk, that most simple and common human activity, can be a sheer joy. Whether we are out for a casual stroll or striding purposefully to some destination, an attitude of ease and appreciation turns walking into a training in the wisdom of mindfulness and healing.

Natural as walking is, bringing full awareness to it or any activity can take some practice. It may be difficult at first to be aware of walking as a continuous stream in which many individual movements and aspects occur separately. At the beginning, choose one distinct aspect of walking, such as the movement of each step, as the focus of concentration. As mindfulness develops, open to the empowering energy of your surroundings: the ground, the air, sounds, smells, and the view. Take pleasure in the seamless interplay of body and mind, and walk, walk, walk.

Among the many walking practices, you may visualize the source of power above your right shoulder and imagine that your walk takes you around this image of peace, in a circumambulation that is a gesture of paying respect to it.

When walking into a house, building, or town, you could pay respect to all beings inside by thinking: "I am entering into the world of suffering beings in order to help them," or, "I am entering into a pure land of the Buddhas." When leaving any place, you could think, "I am leading beings out of suffering," or, "I am thankful for the chance to have seen these beings who are Buddhas."

## SITTING AND STANDING

Sitting is the principal physical posture for meditation, allowing the mind to relax and develop with the least interference. When you are not meditating, good posture and a comfortable position encourage everyday mindfulness. You can also be aware of being firmly seated, which produces a grounded, stable state of mind.

When standing, open your body in a good, relaxed posture, as if an imaginary string at the crown of your head were comfortably pulling you up and properly aligning your spine. This has the practical benefit of reducing fatigue. It also allows you to be more open to other people as you communicate with them. If you must stand in line at the supermarket or a bus stop, try opening your posture. Instead of being bored or frustrated, opening your posture can help you enjoy and open to the precious moment of life unfolding as you wait.

## WORKING

Working consumes most of our waking life. From childhood through early adulthood, we work hard as students year after year. Then we are busy building a career and earning a living. Finally, we retire, and work hard just to survive, to keep body and mind together, and to push away the boredom and isolation of old age. In mundane life there is not much time for anything other than work and sleep.

If we use our work life as a tool for healing, we can transform our lives into an emotional and spiritual gold mine. We can do this by cultivating a peaceful center in ourselves in every situation our work presents.

Whatever we do—office work, gardening, carpentry, painting, or writing—we can use the work as an expression of our peaceful inner nature. Try to find work that is naturally interesting to you, but also try to be interested in any work that you do.

When work is going well, enjoy and celebrate it mindfully. When we feel bored or frustrated, we can bring calm and mindfulness to this too. See all of work as likable, or at least find something likable about it. Enjoy the people you come in contact with, be glad and satisfied at problems being solved. Try to view the struggle of work as a positive challenge, and the negative experiences as an exercise in tolerance and letting go. If we feel trapped by a particular situation, we can tell ourselves: "There's no place else I'd rather be. I like it right here." By saying this with conviction, our spacious nature can open up.

Attitudes such as compassion, and skillful means such as meditation on light, are not intended as airy theories. We can bring them right into our work. In particular, the attitude of openness, as experienced upon awakening or receiving blessings in the morning, can be the foundation for all our working day. With openness, every situation can merge into spiritual experience, like snowflakes falling into the ocean.

## LOOKING

There is more to looking than passively taking in the forms and colors around us. Our eyes are windows through which we project our mental energies. With a single glance, our eyes can communicate kindness and joy. The eyes of a negative person can fill other people with bitterness and pain.

With warm and smiling eyes, let compassion shine out. In this way the act of looking becomes a prayer, a meditation, and a way of healing. If we look at others with kind and caring eyes, we need no other prayers or mental exercises. If we see the outside world with calmness and clarity, our inner being will reflect this positive energy, as in a mirror.

## TALKING

As with the way we look at other people, our words and tone of voice can have a profound impact on the hearts of ourselves and of those around us. So kind, caring speech becomes a prayer. Our everyday speaking voice can be soothing, gentle, strong, and also forthright when necessary. If we feel tongue-tied and unable to communicate with others, we can ask for strength from the source of power and imagine that our speech is purified. Let the sound of your voice ring out confidently, as if it is rising spontaneously from the source of power.

If we habitually speak before we think, this can sow all kinds of trouble for others and ourselves. Think, then speak. And learn to listen. Rather than using conversation as if it were merely an occasion to promote our own agenda, like a prerecorded program, listen openly to what the other person has to say. This seems so obvious, but how many of us really do this? We can develop the gift of listening, which is another way of releasing the grip on self.

## SLEEP

In the most advanced Buddhist training, during sleep the mind merges into a state of luminous clarity, and upon awakening manifests as the transcendental wisdom of awareness, free from grasping at self. It takes a great deal of spiritual experience to extend meditation into sleep, but this is possible with consistent, heart-felt training.

Even if we can't turn sleep into the clear awareness of meditation, some simple Buddhist practices can give us comfort as we fall asleep, and this itself is healing. In a very peaceful way, visualize light. Or visualize with gentle devotion the source of power in the center of your body or above you, illuminating your body with light that radiates outward to the world and universe.

If you would like to extend your training beyond waking consciousness, form the strong intention that you will bring clear awareness of meditation into sleep, and stay with the visualization even as your mind begins to ease into the sleep state. Eventually, if we keep practicing, this enlightened awareness may rise spontaneously within sleep.

If you wake up in the middle of the night, repeat your meditation with a feeling of openness. It is also a good practice if you have insomnia to feel as though you are a body of light. Or ground your scattered thoughts by bringing a gentle awareness to your feet or to the area of your stomach just below the navel, and feel the presence of light there. The relaxed awareness of breathing is also very calming and can usher you safely back to sleep.

## DREAMS AS A MEANS TO AWAKENING

Another Buddhist training involves the contemplation of dreams, both in sleep and in waking life. We normally think of our dreams at night as illusions, but an even greater wisdom is to appreciate waking existence as dream-like and ultimately illusory. Contemplating this truth is a way to soften our everyday attachments and desires.

Thinking about dreams, and how life is like a dream, may open a doorway to the mind in sleep. At bedtime, think again and again: "I will recognize my dreams as dreams, and not be attached to or frightened by them as if they were real." Some meditators are able to bring a nimble awareness to sleep. While dreaming, they recognize the dream as an illusion and so, for example, can fly blissfully above danger or change a demon into a Buddha.

So we recognize dreams as dreams—and waking appearances as dreams too! A deep understanding of this releases our tight cravings and graspings.

For Buddhists, the equanimity this practice brings is considered excellent preparation for the important transition state between life and death. This is also a training that lightens the suffering of our waking existence. Of course, we should maintain our common sense and balance. In Tibet, I remember one misguided person who went to the extreme of slaughtering some cattle, using dream teachings as an excuse. The healthy approach is to develop a playful wisdom about "reality." We are responsible for our actions; the karmic law of causation tells us that. At the same time, it is also quite true that life is changeable, fleeting, and illusory. Great nations and systems rise and fall, people live and die, things are here and then they disappear.

In our own waking existence, we can be more playful in our perceptions of the "real" events pressing in on us. Imagine how they will look in a hundred years, or even a few months or days. Great triumphs and tragedies may seem solid and real today, but with the passage of very little time they take on the quality of interesting fables. So we don't need to take ourselves too seriously. We can relax and at the same time advance along the right path of life.

## A SIMPLE PRACTICE

We may feel so bound by obligations to family, friends, and work from the moment we wake up that it seems difficult to fit in spiritual training. If that is the case, it might be better to have a simple practice in bed before getting up and being distracted by the rush of daily life.

The practice of awakening in openness, as described earlier in this chapter, is an especially fruitful training. The mind is at home in feelings of calm and warmth. Know that you can extend your spacious feelings to every situation.

Starting with a morning practice increases the impact of healing energy, like a morning that begins with a beautiful sunrise.

## THREE IMPORTANT POINTS TO FOCUS ON

What is the best way to live? A very good answer to that question is to place the emphasis on the present moment, just here, right now, the exact point at which we are living and over which we have direct and immediate dominion. So, first of all, seize this very time, and live wisely and well in the present, without losing your focus in the past, future, or somewhere else.

Secondly, we should focus our attention on our own lives and those for whom we have responsibility. By dealing practically with the living beings in our immediate circle, we won't fall into hazy generalizations and dream worlds. Begin now to be a source of happiness to those who are right here every day, including family, friends, neighbors—and yourself.

Thirdly, we should dedicate ourselves to the welfare and happiness of all beings, especially those we are with. This is the essence of spirituality. As the hermit tells the king at the end of Leo Tolstoy's story "The Three Questions":

> Remember then: there is only one important time—*now*. And it is important because it is the only time we have dominion over ourselves; and the most important man is *he with whom you are*, for no one can know whether or not he will ever have dealings with any other man; and the most important pursuit is to *do good to him*, since it is for that purpose alone that man was sent into this life.

# PART THREE

# BUDDHIST
# MEDITATIONS
# THE
# PATH
# TO
# OPENNESS

# 12

# THE MEDITATIONS OF TRANQUILLITY AND INSIGHT ～

THE HEALING EXERCISES in this book are meant to make us happier and more peaceful in our everyday lives. This is a perfectly good goal, but perhaps a limited one, for Buddhists believe that the ultimate healing is to go beyond "my" happiness, to realize the true wisdom and liberation that transcends grasping at thoughts and emotions. These final chapters outline some fundamental meditations that can open us to this realization.

Describing meditation is always difficult, since words can only approximate the actual experience of an individual. Then, too, realization has many stages. It is easy for any meditator, even one with much experience and devotion, to get detoured in grasping of one sort or another. This is why, at a certain point, it can be very important to carefully search out a master for guidance.

For some wise people, any healing exercise or experience could lead to enlightenment. In Tibet, there are stories of beginners who have meditated on "preliminary practices" and experienced the highest realization, while others who practice the most advanced trainings and claim spiritual wisdom may not have a clue to the true meaning of the teachings.

The practices of tranquillity and insight, which are common to all schools of Buddhism, are the well-trodden and proven methods that have the ultimate goal of openness and "selflessness"—freedom from the suffering caused by grasping at self.

Even though these practices could lead to higher realization, they can benefit anyone no matter what his or her state of mind or degree of spirituality is. All the meditations in these final chapters can provide "ordinary" healing and happiness, just as the healing exercises described earlier could in some cases lead to realization.

Although we could train the mind in tranquillity by bringing our full attention to virtually any phenomenon, here the focus is breathing. Our breathing is a simple object of attention, without color or shape. Further, breathing is so intimately interlocked with mind and body that to bring our awareness to it naturally steadies us in mindfulness, and so opens the way to oneness.

In addition to the contemplation of breathing, many schools of Buddhism also rely on powerful visualization practices. But without a doubt, our simple breathing meditation contains the seed of enlightenment. The emphasis is on mindfulness and awareness of breathing, the path to tranquillity and insight.

Tranquillity is the steadying of the mind, the means to oneness, the clearing of muddy waters into openness. Insight is awareness and oneness, the openness itself, without concepts or a separation between a "self" and the object being experienced.

While beginners may spend many months, or even years, training in tranquillity before being comfortable with insight practice, the boundaries between these meditations can be very indistinct. So don't worry too much about definitions. Simply sit in a good posture and practice awareness of breathing.

Especially at first, our mind can seem like such a ragged and disorderly place, disturbed by the slightest sound, thought, or impulse. Seeing the moving, restless character of the mind is the first step toward concentration. By bringing your mind back to your breathing, gradually it can become more steady.

## TRANQUILLITY MEDITATION

Concentration on an object without any wavering is the training of tranquillity. One way to describe this is to say we are concentrating one-pointedly, which means we focus our awareness on only this one object, in this case our breathing. Again and again, gently but firmly bring your awareness to your breathing.

Many beginners find it helpful to concentrate on the breath at one particular place, namely at the tip of the nose or above the upper lip where the breath can be felt. However, you don't need to locate your breathing in this way, as long as you feel relaxed and able to focus your attention.

Another useful device is to count your breaths. In your mind, count "one" as you exhale, "two" as you inhale, and so forth, to "ten." Continue without breaking the series, counting one to ten, repeating the process as long as you are comfortable.

Allowing the abdomen to be relaxed can help you breathe calmly. Some people tend to breathe high in the chest, especially when they are tense. When we breathe naturally, with the abdomen moving softly outward as we inhale, the breath becomes full and relaxed.

While concentrating on breathing, if you feel uneasy—as if your breath is becoming shorter or constricted—then concentrate more on exhaling for a while. Exhaling into infinite space releases the pressure of concentration. Generally, inhalations are shorter than exhalations. After a while, the duration of your breaths will naturally become longer, but you should not make any effort to make them longer.

As your mind steadies and you feel less distracted, bring awareness to your inhaling and exhaling, without counting. Be aware of your breaths as they arise, dwell, and dissolve. This practice of tranquillity makes it easier, outside of meditation, to bring a relaxed mindfulness to whatever we do.

Just when we feel like congratulating ourselves for our wonderful practice of tranquillity, it may suddenly occur to us that we are nearly asleep. Drowsiness is a natural byproduct of the blessing of calmness. Do not be discouraged. But do wake up! It can be a struggle to bring back our dreamy, wandering mind to our breathing. But, without being rigid or aggressive, we should come back to our breathing. Then we can be calm and clear.

During meditation, various subtle and peaceful experiences are possible. You may feel light as a feather. Your whole body may be bathed in bliss, alive with a feeling like the soft, caressing touch of a cool breeze. Some people see lovely images in their mind's eye of stars, the sun and moon, clusters of jewels, garlands of flowers, and so on. If anything like this happens, take it as a sign of progress of concentration. Your meditation can be very joyful, but do not try to cling or hold on to bliss. Trying to capture, "freeze," or duplicate such blissful experiences can become an obstacle to spiritual growth.

## INSIGHT MEDITATION

To experience the true nature of any object of contemplation, just as it is, is the training of insight. Through the contemplation of breathing, we become aware of the movements and subtle nature of breathing, as it is.

Become one in awareness with the breathing. In the oneness of mind and breathing, there is no self to grasp at. This simple realization of the true nature of breathing can help us realize the absolute nature of all phenomena as being without self.

In tranquillity meditation, we follow our breathing, and so must practice focusing on "breathing." In insight practice, we remain in awareness of breathing without thinking about the why or wherefore of it, or any other concepts, such as "feeling the peace of the breathing."

Insight is the practice of clarity in oneness. For example, we may be aware of long breaths, short breaths, beginnings, middles, and endings of breaths, or calmness of breathing. Our breathing comes, goes, and changes, free from attachment or grasping. In awareness there is no need for an "I" to think about or remark on this. Simply be in the awareness of oneness.

One approach to insight meditation is to begin with contemplation of breathing, and at some point to let go of focus or technique. The object of the meditation then is any object that arises, or no object at all. We could be aware of breathing, or we could simply rest in the space that may begin to open up between thoughts.

In this open practice of insight, allow whatever arises in the mind to come and go, without clinging. All kinds of thoughts, feelings, sensations, images, and experiences may arise. Neither push them away nor chase after them. We may feel the intrusion of an "I" that is watching the meditation. However, there is no need to see this as an intrusion; simply let it rise up and dissolve. Let everything be, positive or negative, without attachment. The stillness between thoughts is our open nature. The thoughts as they arise are perfectly fine, but do not grasp after them.

During meditation, we might experience waves of painful feelings, but as we allow them to come, without grabbing at them, they can become peaceful. Imperfection is not a problem when we are open; it is fine just as it is. With the awareness of insight, feelings are neither pleasant nor unpleasant, but are experienced openly, and so transcended.

Practicing the meditation on insight brings the possibility of seeing the momentary character, the selflessness, of the infinite variety and forms of phenomena, at the point of their arising and dissolving. Such a realization lifts the curtain of mental illusions and emotional fabrications from the face of primordial nature of things as they are. Craving for pleasure or aversion to pain, which are rooted in grasping at self, will then spontaneously dissolve like drawings on water.

In meditation, it is possible to see the body as neither pure nor impure, but just as vast expanse. The mind is neither eternal nor nonexistent, but just pure openness. All phenomena are neither with nor without selfhood, a true existence, but are open, peaceful, and free from elaboration.

Any glimpse of openness can help us in our lives. If we have some understanding and experience of openness, it will be wise to deepen and broaden our practice, in meditation and life.

Perhaps the descriptions of insight meditation and openness make realization sound unattainable. Thinking this could be good. Then we could let go of the idea of gaining some "experience" as described in a certain way, and this in itself can help us meditate openly.

# 13

# THE HEALING MEDITATION
# OF DEVOTION ～

EVERYTHING IS ONE in Buddha-nature: the mind, the earth
and stars, time and space. Everything is perfect in this oneness,
even that which we ordinarily see as imperfection. Buddha-nature
is in all living beings, and in the particulars of everyday life. Ultimately, Buddha is beyond images, words, or concepts, which are
creations of dualistic mind.

This is what Buddhists believe. So when some Westerners
become interested in Buddhism, they could be disappointed to
learn about the practice of devotion. They say something like:
"This is what we wanted to leave behind, praying to a high authority outside ourselves." What a funny situation, to run away
from devotion, only to find belief and prayer waiting around the
next corner!

Yes, it's true that the whole universe is Buddha-nature, and
that peace lies within us. So why practice devotion? It is one way
we have of letting go of the idea of self. Belief helps us to open.
It is the releasing of doubts and fears. Being open and receptive
is a way of asking for the help we need.

Certain schools of Buddhism emphasize the act of bowing

as a devotional practice. This is a simple way of surrendering self. It acknowledges the belief that grasping and trying to control everything leads us away from wisdom. Belief is also possible outside of institutional religion. For example, the Twelve Steps program of Alcoholics Anonymous emphasizes giving up the tight little "I" that tries to control. It acknowledges the need for help from a "higher power," in whatever way that is understood by the individual.

In Buddhism, devotion is the development of trust in the Buddha as guide; trust in the Dharma, the teachings of Buddhism, as the path; and trust in the Sangha, the Buddhist community, as support on the spiritual journey.

Devotion means asking for strength along the path. The fulfillment of our spiritual needs may not always be in the form we desire or expect, or according to our timetable. The important point of belief is openness; that is the way to receive blessings and relieve suffering. Quoting Guru Padmasambhava, Paltrül Rinpoche writes:

> If your mind is free from doubts, wishes will be achieved.
> If you have total trusting devotion, blessings will enter you.

Devotion is like the sun, melting our grasping at self and allowing our true nature to shine through. Quoting Drigung Kyobpa Rinpoche, Paltrül Rinpoche writes:

> From the snow-mountain-like master . . . ,
> Without the touch of the rays of sunlike devotion
> The streamlike blessing will not flow.
> So exert your mind in the training of devotion.

If we do not have trust or devotion, even if the Buddha is standing in front of us in person, we will receive hardly any benefits, for our minds, which are the only key to our spiritual growth, are not ready for the opportunity. That is why a Tibetan proverb says:

From whomever one sees as a Buddha
The blessings are received as from a Buddha.
From whomever one sees as a fool
The effects come as from a fool.

So the Buddha-nature is everywhere, but it is possible to train in devotion by meditating upon the Buddha, for instance in the form of a statue or a mental image. The statue itself will not change our lives, it is our minds that can open through the act of devotion. This is the essence of skillful means. Spiritual objects can inspire us, but the main factor is not any object. It is the way we see it, positively, and the way we feel, with devotion and trust, that help us along the path.

Relying on any spiritual object or mental image is a way to empower ourselves with the joy that arises from the Buddha within us all.

Until now, I have emphasized how anyone can meditate upon a source of power of his or her own choosing, such as the sun, the moon, or some personal image. But here I will describe a source of power that is specifically Buddhist, a devotional meditation upon Guru Rinpoche Padmasambhava, the ninth-century founder of Tibetan Buddhism who embodies all the enlightened ones—Buddhas, divinities, saints, and sages.

There are so many spiritual representations that could inspire us as a source of power. We could, for example, meditate upon Shakyamuni Buddha to help us gain wisdom; or the Medicine Buddha for healing; or Tara, the Buddha in female form, for pacifying all fears and dangers. I have chosen Guru Rinpoche because of his boundless compassion, which has helped so many people over the centuries who have called upon him, and because I myself trained in his lineage. Guru Rinpoche's majestic presence is the vajra manifestation of absolute Buddhahood, the overwhelming strength and bliss of the universe that pacifies all turmoil.

As background to this meditation, I will go into quite a bit of detail about how we might visualize the image of Guru Rinpoche. Every detail of the iconography associated with a sacred image gives a teaching, and these signs, symbols, colors, and gestures can arouse positive feelings in us that mirror those teachings, both one by one, and as they are seen and felt as part of a whole.

Details can help an experienced meditator rest in awareness of a mental image that is full and rich. But don't worry if you lack experience and skill; simply visualize however much you feel comfortable with. In the following guided meditation, what really matters is the feelings the words attempt to convey. Use the feelings to call up in your mind an image of Padmasambhava that is simple but heartfelt. If you merely feel the warmth and presence of Padmasambhava, that in itself can be very healing.

Remember, too, that artistic renderings such as those in this book are meant as an aid. A picture or statue may inspire you, teach you, or help as a starting point for meditation, but don't feel limited by it. What matters in visualization is the image in your own mind, and the warmth and openness that can come through devotion.

## INVOKING THE MAJESTIC IMAGE OF PADMASAMBHAVA

Like a flower that blossoms from emptiness, the majestic presence of Padmasambhava arises from the imagination. In an aura of beautiful light, the radiant and youthful Guru Rinpoche sits on a clear, shining moon disc, above a bright, warm sun disc. The moon and sun are resting just above a huge lotus plant, fragrant and perfumed, fresh with moisture. The lotus has thousands of brilliantly colored petals.

The sun, moon, and lotus are symbols of his birth. He was born by "immaculate birth" in the "Lotus Buddha Family" out of the union of wisdom (sun) and compassion (moon).

*Padmasambhava, also known as Guru Rinpoche*

Guru Rinpoche's face is white with a reddish hue, ever youthful and wise, beyond the realm of change and aging. His smile of joy is beyond suffering. His clear, unblinking, loving eyes bring universal bliss, healing our mind in its every movement and mood and our body in every cell and atom.

His robes radiate light. His white inner robe and red gown symbolize the enlightenment of a bodhisattva, who helps all suffering beings in this world. His blue outer gown symbolizes the perfection of the esoteric attainments, and he wears the shawl of perfect monkhood. A brocade cloak is a symbol that all religious trainings are one in universal truth. This cloak, and his hat and shoes, are also reminders of his mystical powers. They are gifts from a King of Zahora who was amazed at his powers. The king had tried to burn him, but Guru Rinpoche simply transformed the fire into water, now known as Rewalsar Lake in India.

Guru Rinpoche holds the symbols of the teachings. A golden vajra in his right hand symbolizes indestructible skill and power, the masculine principle. In his left hand he cradles a skull, which holds a vase filled with the nectar of immortality. The skull symbolizes the union of emptiness and bliss, which are the feminine principle. The vase and nectar symbolize long life and the timeless truth of the Buddha-nature.

In Buddhism, esoteric masters are often spiritually united with a female consort. The wisdom of femininity is represented here by a trident, which rests in the fold of Guru Rinpoche's left arm. The three sharp points of the trident signify the three true natures of the mind: openness, clarity, and the power of compassion. Three heads ornament the trident, representing the three Buddha-bodies: the skeletal head is total openness, the mature image is the pure form of the Buddha as it is, and the youth is the impure image of Buddha as seen by ordinary minds.

Among the other symbols are locks of hair hanging from the trident. These are a reminder of the practice in charnel grounds of meditating upon the dissolution of the body, and the liberation of realizing the truth of living and dying.

In his limitless wisdom, Guru Rinpoche knows every happening in the universe, simultaneously and without distracting from his absolute, open nature. His infinite compassion is open to the whole universe and reaches every single being, as a mother showers her only child with love.

Now that we have some familiarity with this image, here is an extended devotional meditation.

## CALLING UPON THE STRENGTH AND COMPASSION OF PADMASAMBHAVA

Visualize that you are sitting at some lofty spot such as a mountaintop, looking at the vast, clear blue sky. Enjoy the view for a few minutes, resting in the openness. The image of being at a high spot raises your mind above your own turmoil. The open sky clears your mind of the images, thoughts, and emotions that constantly crowd it.

From this openness, first imagine the lotus seat with its beautiful petals, then the sun disc, and above it the moon disc. Finally, Guru Rinpoche radiantly appears.

Feel the boundless peace and warmth of this loving divinity, and rest comfortably for some time in those feelings. Allow devotion to melt your heart. As you bring your awareness to the image, give yourself wholly to it, not just as a form created by your mind, but as the true and pure healing Guru.

Now imagine the whole earth filled with all kinds of beings with devotional hearts, cheerful faces, and joyful eyes. All are looking at the loving, beautiful, and powerful face of Guru Rinpoche, the source of all healing. Imagine that you hear them all saying a mantra in one voice, in a thunderous and sweet melody. The mantra is a prayer to Guru Rinpoche, a means of healing our problems, a joyous expression of mental and physical energies, a celebration of the presence of this divinity, a meditation on pure sound that is in itself the nature of oneness.

From the depths of your heart, chant the mantra of Guru Rinpoche, in either of the forms that follow:

### In Tibetanized Sanskrit

OM   AH   HUNG   BEDZAR   GURU   PEMA   SIDDHI   HUNG

### In Sanskrit

OM   AH   HUM   VAJRA   GURU   PADMA   SIDDHI   HUM

A translation of this is: "The embodiment of the body, speech, and mind of the Buddhas, O Padma[sambhava], please grant all blessings."

As a result of the prayers and openness, beams of blessing lights of various colors from Guru Rinpoche touch you, bringing warmth and openness in body and mind. These lights are not just beautiful, pure forms but the energy of peace, warmth, bliss, and openness. Allow this feeling to pervade you, through every pore and door, dispelling all worry and distress, as sunlight dispels darkness. Feel that your whole body is transformed into light and healing energy.

Repeat the mantra many times, giving yourself wholly to the sound. Imagine that your prayers have opened the minds of all beings to devotional joy, and the light from Guru Rinpoche radiates in every direction, dispelling all the confusion, sadness, and pain. All beings are liberated in a mighty chorus of chanting. The chant fills the universe, which becomes one in sound, light, and joy.

Rejoice in this warmth and openness. Allow all concepts and feelings to merge into an ocean of devotional peace, in which there are no distinctions or boundaries, beyond pain and excitement, good and bad, this and that, you and me, but where all are one and the same.

Although the higher purpose of this meditation is spiritual realization, you could also contemplate Guru Padmasambhava as the source of power for ordinary healing of emotional or physical problems, by visualizing any form of healing energy emanating from the image, such as laser-like light. Or imagine healing nectar from Guru Rinpoche's vase flowing into you, first washing away all your mental, emotional, and physical suffering, then filling your whole body and mind with peace and strength. Guru Rinpoche could also be the source of energy during meditations in which another person acts as a healer for you.

Whatever the visualization, you can repeat it during one session as often as it feels comfortable. When you are doing your daily chores, from time to time bring the open feeling of the meditation into your life. You can even chant the mantra out loud, or silently when you're in public.

## MEDITATING IN OPENNESS

In the higher Buddhist view, appearances rise from emptiness, and dissolve back again. So we began this devotional meditation by entering the state of openness, letting the visualization arise like a reflection in a clear mirror. After resting in tranquillity upon the imagery, we end in openness and oneness again. It is a process like birth, living, and dying, a good way to practice letting come and go. Always, at the end of meditation, simply be in the openness of your state of mind, just as it is, without grasping.

Depending on our state of mind, we may rest longer and longer in the space of openness. We may begin with a visualization, and then drop technique and simply meditate in an open way. Then it doesn't matter so much what the experience of meditation is. It may be possible to merge the experience, the experiencer, and the ways of experiencing all into oneness.

Don't try to shape the openness, or see it as one thing or another, or gain anything from it. Just let things be. This is the way to find your center. If you trust your true nature, you do not need to look for another center. Just be open and aware.

As long as we are subject to the possibility of suffering, meditation can deepen and strengthen us. As we realize the nature of openness, meditation melts into everyday life.

Relying on external healing sources is helpful and even essential as long as we are under the control of dualistic concepts and depend on external objects. However, it is important to understand that the ultimate healing is going beyond dependence on external forces. It is securing our own peaceful, openness nature so that we can reach all through that peace and openness.

# 14

# AWAKENING THE INFINITE INNER ENERGIES OF HEALING ~~~

TAKING ONE or two deep breaths, release all your stress and worries and enjoy the relaxed feelings in your body and mind. Then slowly and calmly go through the following exercises, taking a minute or two for each step.

1. When you wake up in the morning, or at any time of the day, feel devotion to the source of power. (It could be the Buddha, Guru Rinpoche, or any other source of power.) Devotion wakes up your body and mind and makes them blossom. Devotion brings warmth, bliss, strength, and openness.

2. Visualize and feel that your heart, the center of your body, is in the form of an amazing flower of light, blossoming in the warmth of devotion. As a result, from that devotional flower-heart arises your wisdom, compassion, and power, the enlightened qualities in the form of the source of power. The source of power, in the form of a light body with heat and bliss, rises up through the central channel—a spacious channel made of clear and pure light—of your body. Then the source of power adorns the stainless and limitless sky, as if thousands of suns have arisen as one body.

3. Believe that the source of power is the embodiment of wisdom, compassion, and power of all the divinities and of the universal truth. Feel that your whole body and mind are filled with heat, bliss, and boundless energy by being in the presence of the source of power.

4. Then see that the whole earth is filled with various beings. Their hearts are filled with devotion and their faces are blossoming with joyful smiles. Their wide-open eyes are one-pointedly watching the source of power with wonder. Joining you, they are all expressing the power of their devotion in prayers, singing harmoniously with various resonances, like a great symphony. Sing the prayer with great celebration in which there are no limits or restrictions.

5. Singing the prayers, imagine that the prayers have invoked the compassionate mind of the source of power. From the source of power, its wisdom, compassion, and power come toward you in the form of multiple beams of blessing lights of various colors (or streams of nectar). These beams of light touch every pore of your body. Feel the heat of their mere touch. Feel the blissful nature of the heat. And feel the power of the blissful heat.

6. Then the beams of light enter your body. Visualize and feel that all your negative habits, mental ills, emotional conflicts, lack of fulfillment, fear, physical sicknesses, and circulation or energy blockages are in the form of darkness in your body. By the mere touch of the blessing light, all the darkness is completely dispelled, without any trace, from your body and mind. Your body is filled with amazing bright light, with the sensation of heat, bliss, and strength. Then see and feel that your whole body is transformed into a blessing light body. Feel that every cell of your body is transformed into the cells of blessing light with heat, bliss, and strength.

7. Then think of a cell on your forehead (or any other place in your body). The cell is made of bright blessing light. It is vast

*Awakening*
*the Infinite*
*Inner*
*Energies of*
*Healing*

175

and beautiful. Slowly, enter into the cell. It is limitless and boundless as the sky. Feel the vastness of the cell for a while.

8. Then see and feel that your body is made of billions of the same kind of vast, beautiful, blissful cells. Each cell is adorned with the presence of the source of power. Be aware of the amazing display and energy of your miraculous body. All the cells are in love and harmony with each other. Feel the power of these billions of blissful cells in your body adorned by the sources of power.

9. All the cells of the channels, organs, and muscles of your blessing light body are breathing. They are breathing heat and bliss openly and spontaneously like the waves of the ocean. Feel the waves of blissful movement. The waves caress, relax, and melt any place where we have hardness or rigidity, any fixations of unresolved emotions and unhealed wounds with their traces. Feel the energy aura. Feel the feeling. Be one with the feeling.

10. Then you could sing OM, AH, and HUNG (see pages 125–126 and 136–138) as the healing movement to generate strength and openness and unite with them. You can sing loudly, softly, or silently in your mind.

As you repeatedly sing OM slowly and continuously, be aware of how the waves of sound powerfully resonate in every cell, from your vocal cords through your whole body like the waves of the ocean. Delight in the feeling of power and strength, the qualities of the Buddha-body.

In the same way, singing AH, be aware of the opening, releasing, and blossoming energies, the qualities of the Buddha-speech.

Singing HUNG, be aware of merging yourself with the union of power and openness, which is the boundless power, the qualities of the Buddha-mind.

11. You could also make gestures with your hands as healing movements (see pages 136–138) to generate strength and openness and unite with them.

Extremely slowly and continuously, fold your fingers into

vajra-fists at your heart by pressing the base of the ring fingers with the tips of the thumbs and then folding the rest of the fingers over the thumbs, with the index and little fingers slightly open and facing up. Place your feet at the point where the hips join the thighs. Be aware of how the movement reverberates from every cell of your hands through your body like the flow of a river. Delight in the feel of power and strength, the qualities of the Buddha-body.

In the same way, make a gesture of a blossoming flower at your heart. Holding the fists upward, unfold the fingers of your fist (one after another, starting with the little fingers) and open your hands and arms—and be aware of the delightful feeling of opening, releasing, and blossoming, the qualities of the Buddha-speech.

Make a contemplative gesture, placing your hands palms up in your lap, the right hand over the left hand, with the thumbs slightly touching, and be aware of merging yourself with the union of power and openness, which is the boundless power, the qualities of the Buddha-mind.

You could also perform these gestures while singing OM, AH, and HUNG.

12. You could see an amazingly vast aura of bright blessing light filled with energy power around your body. It is a protective aura that prevents any negative effects from coming in. It is also an aura of transmutation that transforms everything in the energy aura into blessing light, like snowflakes falling into warm water.

Share the blessings with all mother-beings.

# 15

# THE HEALING MEDITATION OF COMPASSION ～

IF WE DEVELOP compassion, other spiritual experiences will naturally rise within us. Compassion is the root of all virtues. It can free us from grasping at self.

We are all capable of tremendous, unstinting, big-hearted compassion, because of the Buddha-nature that is always present within us. Compassion opens our closed, rigid minds. It calms our wild temper and transforms our dank, rotting, negative disposition. It brings us out of darkness, the hidden jail created by our selfish and frustrated existence, into the daylight. Instead of sucking from everyone else to feed our wild ego, we can find our true center through compassion for others. Compassion is the healing nature of our mind, through which we can find peace.

Even if we understand that compassion puts us squarely on the true path, we can find it hard to stop clinging to our own selfish concerns long enough so that we experience openness toward others. The basic approach in Buddhism is to begin in a simple way, and open the circle of our compassion outward.

So we should feel a healthy sense of love for ourselves, taking care of our true needs and welfare, and welcome joy when it rises within us. We should appreciate those near to us and care about them, gaining firsthand experience of a warmhearted attitude, rather than relying on mere words or vague feelings. Gradually, we can extend our practice of compassion.

Compassion does not mean worrying. It is openhearted wisdom and caring. Worrying, on the other hand, is rooted in grasping. It saps our strength and ability to help others.

Often, when we care for someone, we worry. This is the unavoidable reaction of the mundane mind. So, if you can, care, but don't worry. If worries erupt anyway, don't worry about worrying. Rather, see this as positive, and think: "I am worrying because of my love for this person. Caring is the best attitude." By seeing the worry in this positive light and rejoicing over it, the negative impact will be transformed into constructive energy.

How can we feel compassion toward our enemies or people we don't like? The effective approach is to see them as mother-beings, who are actually kind, good, and loving, except that their true nature is obscured; or perhaps we find it difficult to recognize the Buddha within them because of our own clouded vision.

In meditation, we can begin to break down the walls that separate us from others. Tsongkhapa says this about compassion and meditation:

> The characteristic of compassion is the thought, "May all beings become free from sufferings," and "I will lead them to freedom." The stages of compassion are that first one should meditate on loved ones, then on neutral people, and then on enemies. When one has the compassion that views enemies and loved ones equally, meditate on all the beings of the universe.

I am going to describe a mental exercise that focuses graphically on the anguish of others. Some people worry that meditating on terrible suffering might cause mental illness, but actually it heals us by releasing the grip on our own ego. So open your heart, and allow the feeling of compassion to well up.

Vividly visualize and empathize with a being who is helpless, terrified, tortured, and crying for help. You could use the image of a person who is dying alone in excruciating pain with no hope of surviving, who every second hangs on to the hope of surviving, crying for help and staring at the world of the living with a stream of tears. Or you could visualize someone who is being dragged to his death by the rough hands of executioners in front of the fearful, weeping eyes of helpless loved ones. Or see a harmless, gentle animal who is being slaughtered with the sharp knives of butchers amid the thunder of terrifying laughter. Or imagine a person who is trapped in a fire, flood, or earthquake, glancing at the ever-cherished world for the last time through bloodstained tears.

Then understand that this suffering being is none other than your own parent, child, or loved one, for Buddhists believe all beings have been our loved ones, at one time or another, during our exceedingly numerous past lives. Then think, "When she was my mother, she gave all the love and care that I needed, she warmed my heart with her kindness and sacrificed her happiness and sleep for my sake, always thinking of me. But today no one will help her escape from this danger. She has no chance to develop the wisdom and strength she needs at this last moment. How could I, her only child, spend all my energy on the silly diversions of this life, indifferent to her pain and fear?" Now decide to follow the path of compassion, by thinking, "From this very moment I swear in front of the whole world to dedicate every minute of my life to developing spiritually in order to heal all my suffering mother-beings."

You could also start training in compassion by dwelling on positive images. Think of the kindness and compassion a parent, friend, or mentor has shown to you, and call up the wonderful feeling of warmth those memories give you. Then tell yourself you will pass on this great gift of compassion to others, and give it freely, like light that warms the whole world and universe.

Or you could use your own deeply felt pain and fear to generate compassion. Most of us vainly try to hide from suffering when it comes our way, but it can be an invaluable resource. With the right attitude, the bitter taste of suffering makes it easier to understand the pain of others.

Seeing and feeling suffering brings a strong understanding of *samsara*, our transitory earthly existence. This can generate a powerful energy, not just pity or well-wishes for others, but a wholehearted aspiration and commitment to take responsibility for liberating all beings from the fire pit of samsara.

By developing strong compassion for all our mother-beings, we will lose our hatred, jealousy, envy, and craving. Compassion melts the wall that separates friend and enemy, you and me, good and bad. It allows space for joy and peace.

Asanga, the great Mahayana philosopher of ancient India, contemplated Maitreya, the Buddha of Loving-kindness, in a cave for twelve years. Yet he failed to see any sign of true accomplishment until the day he left the cave and saw a howling, enraged dog dying on the road. As he attempted to help the creature, boundless compassion suddenly welled up, and the dog was transformed into the radiant body of Maitreya. "Lord, you have little compassion," lamented Asanga. "Why didn't you show your face to me for so long?" Maitreya said: "I was always with you without separation. But you couldn't see me because of your own mental obscurations. Compassion purified them all."

As our compassion grows, it becomes easier to let go of the struggles of our continually discriminating minds. In the openness of compassion, we can transform our confusions into pure perception, the mind's primordial wisdom. Most of us find it hard to conceive of realizing lasting, total openness. Yet if we practice compassion, our delusions, attachments, and the habits of bad karma will begin to fall away.

When we become Buddha, compassion spontaneously arises in us as the all-pervading, omnipresent power of Buddhahood. As Longchen Rabjampa says:

From the true nature [Buddhahood],
In all directions, arises the power of compassion,
Accomplishing the prosperity of others through its play.

## INVOKING THE BUDDHA OF COMPASSION TO OPEN OUR HEARTS

Meditating upon any source of power can help us to open to compassion, like the sowing of seeds in fertile ground. It is especially powerful to contemplate a divinity as the image of inspiration. The particular exercise I will describe calls upon Avalokiteshvara, the Buddha of Compassion. The approach and content of this visualization are similar to other exercises that can lead us to openness. The key here is the intention to open our hearts. Even if we sometimes find it hard in everyday life to feel compassion, the intention itself is very healing.

Call up this visualization in however much detail as you comfortably can, contemplating the imagery with a relaxed but heartfelt concentration. Give yourself to the meditation, so that awareness and image are one.

Imagine you are at a high place such as a mountain, looking at the limitless sky. Take a deep breath, and stay in this openness for however long you want, releasing all your stress and worries.

Avalokiteshvara emerges from the open sky in front of you, in the most inspiring, peaceful, and enchanting form you can imagine. His body is white, radiant with light, like a snowy or crystal mountain touched by the rays of thousands of suns.

He is adorned with silks and jewels, and sits upon a moon disc, which rests in the middle of a beautiful lotus. The Buddha is firmly seated, symbolizing the unmoving state of Buddhahood.

In this meditation, the Buddha is endowed with four arms, which dispense boundless compassion to every being in the universe. His first two hands are folded together at his heart in a gesture that symbolizes the oneness of nirvana and samsara—the union of enlightenment with the suffering of the world, the per-

*Avalokiteshvara*

fection of everything as it is, including mundane struggles and impermanence. In his folded hands, he holds a wish-fulfilling jewel, which represents the "skillful means" that fulfill the needs of all beings who are open to the opportunity. The divinity's second right hand holds a crystal rosary to symbolize the constancy of his compassion for all. His second left hand holds a white lotus to symbolize his unstained, boundless knowledge and wisdom.

His eyes are full of infinite kindness and caring, and look at everyone without blinking, in unconditioned and unceasing love. He is both youthful and ageless, beyond all suffering, and his joyful, smiling face brings release from suffering to everyone.

Develop the feeling in your heart that this is not just a form created by your mind, but the true and pure form of the Buddha of Compassion, the embodiment of all Buddhas and enlightened beings. Trust in this image as the reflection of the pure nature of your own mind, which has appeared as the Buddha. Feel his presence in your heart, body, and mind. Rejoice in the blessings he brings to the place where you live, the people you are with, the whole universe.

On the ground facing Avalokiteshvara, visualize all sorts of beings who are overjoyed to be in the presence of the Buddha. Now, with a feeling of warmth, think that all the beings on earth are joining you in chanting the following mantra:

OM   MANI   PADME   HUNG   HRI

*or*

OM   MANI   PADME   HUNG

This can be translated as "Buddha of the Jewel and Lotus, we invoke you," or more broadly as "O Buddha who holds the jewel and lotus of compassion and wisdom, please grant us your blessings."

Give yourself completely to the sound of the chant; say or sing it again and again, in a way that you find inspiring. As you do so, refresh your visualization. With warmth and devotion, imagine that all beings everywhere are looking with wide, joyful eyes at the Buddha. The sweet sound of the mantra fills the universe in a symphony that transforms every form, sound, and concept into a celebration of the Buddha of Compassion.

Now in your mind hear the soothing voice of the Buddha, who is saying again and again: "All your unwholesome actions and feelings are totally and completely healed. Now you are pure and perfect. Feel happiness and peace." Allow the meaning of these words to sink into your heart, not just as words that come and go, but as a true and deeply felt empowerment and blessing.

Now beams of healing light blaze from Avalokiteshvara, and as they touch you, your heart opens fully to all the mother-beings that surround the divinity. These lights are not just beautiful, pure forms but the energy of peace, warmth, bliss, and openness. The light from the Buddha flows through you, to all beings, dispelling all pain and suffering. Allow a feeling of calm and openness to spread through you. Feel that the whole world has become one in compassion. The ice-like coldness and hardness of your untamed mind melts, and by the power of the Buddha's compassionate light your own body is transformed into pure light. The light of the Buddha is like a thousand suns, but it never hurts anyone's eyes; instead it brings a soothing feeling of peace and release. As this infinite light radiates in every direction, the universe merges in peace and oneness.

Feel the vastness and openness of the universe. Allow all your thoughts and feelings to vanish into the Buddha's infinite peace and warmth, in whose compassion there is no distinction between pain and pleasure, good and bad, this and that, you and me. All are one and the same in great peace. Rest in the openness of your healing mind. You may then repeat this meditation again and again, as often as it is comfortable.

This meditation can be varied by using other forms of healing energy as discussed earlier in this book. Karma Chakme, the great master of liturgy, condenses many practices of the common and sacred scriptures, as well as the mystical teachings, in a meditation upon the Buddha of Compassion that can be used to heal ordinary sickness.

Imagine the divinity above the head of the sick person, who could be yourself or someone else. Here the Buddha of Compassion is envisioned with two arms, his right hand offered in protective gesture, his left hand holding a white lotus at his heart. Among the many aspects of his wondrous appearance is the vision of his mantra, OM MANI PADME HUNG, moving in a circle around his heart. Glorious light radiates from the mantra.

Pray to the Buddha of Compassion, the great bodhisattva, provider of fearlessness. Ask for freedom from sickness, and believe that this prayer will be answered.

The rest of the meditation is described by Karma Chakme as follows:

From the body of the Buddha a stream of nectar descends, and washes away all the sickness and ill effects of the sick person, and then nectar-of-bliss fills his or her body.

Then repeat the following mantra as many times as you can: "OM MANI PADME HUNG SARVA SHANTING KURUYE SOHA."*

Then the Buddha above the person's head dissolves into light and merges into the sick person.

Remember that you can always bring the feeling and energy from any meditation on compassion into your daily life; it is a blessing always available to us. Welcome everything life brings you—it is all an opportunity to realize our true nature.

When you are happy, feel it fully as the blessing energy of the Buddha, without grasping at it. When you suffer, think: "May this pain be a ransom to relieve the pain of all beloved mother-beings," and consider the suffering as a positive force that brings spiritual inspiration and awareness, the supreme goal of human life.

---

*"O Buddha of Compassion and Wisdom, may all [these sicknesses] be pacified."

# SCRIPTURAL SOURCES FOR THIS BOOK ～

THE PROBLEMS we face are here and now, but so often the best advice for our difficulties comes down to us from the past. One of my intentions in liberally quoting the great spiritual teachers of the near and distant past is to let these wise voices speak directly, in their own beautiful and inspiring words.

Another reason is to authenticate the basic approach of this book. The scriptures are overflowing with teachings on how our minds can heal suffering. Yet only a small corner of these scriptures can fit into the chapters of a book like this one. I thought readers might be curious to see some healing exercises as they appear in the scriptures. This appendix also presents further scriptural sources about the mind and emotions.

## HEALING THROUGH VISUALIZATION

The scriptures advise us to heal mind and body with strong belief, heartfelt prayer, and the calling up of mental images.

The first step is to identify the mental or physical sickness—

what the Buddhist texts refer to as the "object of negation." Negative emotions and sickness are rooted in grasping at self, but before we can pacify them, it is necessary to see them clearly. As Shantideva says:

> Without identifying the imputed entity,
> You will not realize the nonexistence of it.

So before visualizing a positive image, we need to understand the mind and the source of the trouble. As Zhabkarpa says:

> If you do not ascertain what are the actual characteristics of
>    the mind,
> Whatever virtuous trainings you pursue will not hit the point.
> It is like having the target nearby but
> Shooting the arrow far away.
> It is like having the thief in your house and
> Making a vigorous search outside.

Many texts recommend visualizing the sickness in a form such as dirt. Once the negative image has been called up, it can be purified with healing energies such as nectar and light. Dri-me Özer describes the following visualization, in which the source of power is the Vajrasattva Buddha, the embodiment of infinite truth and strength:

> Think that from the body of the Buddha beams of light and streams of nectar descend into you. The obscurations of your body are purified. . . . Your body is blessed as the vajra body, the body of the Buddha. By the beams of light and streams of nectar from the speech of the Buddha, the defilements of your speech are purified. . . . Your speech is blessed as the vajra speech. By the lights and nectar from the mind of the Buddha the obscurations of your mind are purified. . . . Your mind is blessed as the vajra mind. By the lights and nectar descending from all parts of the Buddha the defilements of grasping at the body, speech and mind as an individual entity ["self"] are purified. . . . You have received the vajra-wisdom blessing.

In a liturgy on healing, Do Khyentse presents a healing visualization that employs smoke, fire, air, water, and nectar:

> The hand of the deity [source of power] holds a wish-fulfilling
>     treasure vase,
> Emitting clouds of fragrant smoke.
> It burns all our impurities, defects, and defilements.
> From the nose of the deity issues wisdom-air,
> Which blows away all our defilements, depression, and
>     cloudiness.
> From the mouth of the deity come blessing mist, cloud,
> And a rain of wisdom nectar, which
> Wash all our sicknesses, demonic effects, defilements,
>     disharmony and dissatisfactions.
> May all the impurities be burnt by the wisdom fire.
> May they be blown away by the powerful force of air.
> May they be purified by the nectar.

Tsewang Chokdrub, a great writer of meditation technique in the eighteenth century, wrote about the need to prepare the mind for healing—particularly through concentration that leads to calm and clear awareness.

> So in order to dispel dullness, you should hold and concentrate
> your mind vigorously, totally, and one-pointedly at the heart.
> In order to dispel laxity, excitement, or wildness of mind, you
> should hold and concentrate your mind vigorously, totally, and
> one-pointedly below the navel. When your concentration be-
> comes one-pointed and strong, there will be neither dullness
> nor excitement in your mind.

One of the actual healing exercises prescribed by Tsewang Chokdrub involves visualizing ourselves as a Buddha and imagining in our hearts the letter HUNG, which represents the Buddha's enlightened mind:

> For healing physical sickness, first visualize and see yourself
> as the deity. At the heart, visualize a dark blue HUNG syllable the
> size of a grain. If the nature of your sickness is heat, visualize that

*The Tibetan letter* HUNG

a white HUNG syllable the size of a grain shoots from the dark blue HUNG syllable, and by encircling every part of your upper body it attracts all the sickness, as a magnet attracts metal, and exits from the top of the skull and disappears in space. Then exhale. If the nature of your sickness is cold, visualize that a red HUNG syllable shoots from the dark blue HUNG and, by encircling every part of your lower body, attracts like a magnet all the sickness related to cold and exits from the "lower doors" and disappears deep down in the earth. If you have pain in a particular place such as the arm, visualize a black HUNG syllable at the place of pain. It attracts all the pain and exits from the tip of your fingers or from your eyes and disappears into space.

Tsewang Chokdrub also describes the approach of merging our awareness into oneness with suffering. He speaks of dissolving into the Great Seal, a Buddhist term for openness.

Whatever sickness you are experiencing or from whatever causes and conditions it has arisen, all the sufferings such as sickness and pain happening to your illusory body are happening because of the chain of delusions that is created by not realizing the truth, that the sufferings have arisen solely because of the action of grasping at self, which is followed by the forces of emotional afflictions, attachment, and hatred. Then you should analyze further. If you are saying, "The root of all these pains and sufferings is grasping at self, and I will renounce it," then the [so-called] renouncer itself is arising as grasping at self. The correct way of renouncing the grasping at self is as follows: whatever pain or sickness you are experiencing, without any fabrications contemplate the union or oneness of [the one who is experiencing] the taste of the pain and the pain itself without accepting [oneself, who is experiencing it] and without rejecting [the pain]. Having concentrated your mind forcefully and one-pointedly on that union, which is unrestricted oneness and openness, both the pain itself and the concept of oneself, who is experiencing the pain, dissolve into the expanse of the Great Seal without any distinction of accepting self and rejecting the pain. This will cut off the ties to grasping at self.

## AWARENESS OF BODY, MIND, AND PHENOMENA

Awareness of the qualities and the nature of your own body, feelings, thoughts, and phenomena are the central focus/theme of the common Buddhist meditations, such as the "contemplation in the Fourfold Mindfulness" and the "tranquillity and insight." It is to maintain the awareness of every mental thought and feeling, and every physical presence and moment, openly, without any conceptual grasping or emotional conflict.

Awareness of the positive and joyful qualities and openness nature of the body, mind and universe are the path and goal of the "two stages" of esoteric Buddhist training.

## REALIZING EVERY CELL OR ATOM OF THE BODY AND OF THE WORLD AS BUDDHA QUALITIES

In esoteric Buddhist teachings, you train in realizing all aspects of your own body and mind and the universe as various Buddha qualities and wisdoms. Even in common teachings they realize every atom as the infinite and limitless display of Buddha pure lands. The *Bhadracharya-pranidhana* says,

> May I realize in each atom
> The perfect array of all the pure lands of the three times.
> May I enter into the pure lands of the Buddhas
> [Of each atom] of all directions.

## UNDERSTANDING THE MIND

Chandrakirti, a great Buddhist Middle Way philosopher of the seventh century, writes:

> Beings, first attaching to "self" as "I," and
> Then to "things" as "my,"
> Revolve in the cycle of mundane life like an irrigation wheel.

But how can we suffering beings loosen attachment to self? Although we tend to think of experiences as positive or negative, the good or bad character of situations does not matter so much as how skillfully we see and use them. Quoting Longchen Rabjam, Paltrül Rinpoche advises us in the use of skillful means to transform our lives.

> Sometimes look at the nature of self-appearing harmonious circumstances.
> By realizing them as self-appearing, they arise as the support of spiritual experiences.
> Sometimes look at the appearances of negative circumstances;
> It is very effective for repelling attachment to the delusions.
> Sometimes look at friends and teachers;
> It inspires you to train by learning their good and bad natures.
> Sometimes look at the display of miracles of the four elements in space;
> It brings the realization of the dissolution of mental efforts in the true nature of the mind.

Sometimes look at the character of your country, dwelling, and
  possessions;
Seeing them as illusions repels your attachment to those
  delusory appearances. . . .
In brief, appraise the nature or character of the phenomena
  appearing in various capacities;
It destroys your deluded attraction to them as real.

Most of us see loneliness as a negative emotion, but experienced meditators have long recognized that this feeling, in a relaxed mind, can help us dissolve rigid concepts and usher in
deeper contemplation. Paltrül Rinpoche writes:

> If you stay at a place where a feeling of loneliness [or sadness,
> detachment, voidness] comes, the contemplative absorption
> arises in us. As the Lord Milarepa says:
>
>> In the caves of empty valleys, where there are no
>>   people,
>> There is no time for the feeling of loneliness to cease,
>> There is no time to dissociate from the mind of
>>   devotion
>> To the Guru and the Buddhas of the three times.

As we begin to understand the mind, we see that it is not
necessary to grasp at happiness, sadness, or any other mental or
external phenomena. In the Buddhist view, all phenomena are
mere reflections and designations of the mind. Mipham Rinpoche writes:

> So, all are magical displays of the mind.
> If liberated, it is the liberation of the mind, and if bound, it is
>   the bondage of the mind.
> Apart from the mind there is neither liberation nor bondage,
> Neither happiness nor suffering and neither Buddha nor
>   beings.

At the highest levels of understanding, we find peace in the
release from grasping, and our emotional afflictions fall away.

Then the merry-go-round of worldly cravings will cease. Shanti-deva writes:

> When you have realized
> That there is no experiencer of feelings and
> There is no feeling,
> How will your craving [which is the result of feeling] not turn
>  away?

## EMOTIONAL AFFLICTIONS

It is our grasping attitudes that cause our emotional afflictions. According to the scriptures, six afflictions are most troublesome: ignorance, hatred, desire, miserliness, jealousy, and arrogance.

Patience is singled out as an especially potent virtue. It is an attitude of letting be, not rejecting or grasping at a circumstance or emotion, but allowing appearances to rise and dissolve. Shanti-deva writes:

> There is no evil like hatred
> And there is no merit like patience.
> Therefore, by various means
> Dedicate your life to the practice of patience.

The scriptural discourses on right attitude recognize the difficulty most of us have with our emotional afflictions. Begin with something easy, say the scriptures. So, if someone is crawling in the thorny nest of jealousy, the first small step is to think of someone less fortunate than ourselves and wish him or her prosperity. This can soften the previously rock-hard habit of wanting only happiness for ourselves and plant the possibility of feeling joy for the good fortune of others.

The advice is often quite down to earth. To loosen the tightness of miserliness, the Buddha himself recommended that people first give others something small, like vegetables. Shanti-deva writes:

The leader [Buddha] introduces people,
At the beginning, to the giving of things such as vegetables.
Having trained gradually, later on,
They will be able to give even their own flesh.

Buddhists believe in the possibility of rebirth and see gener-

osity as creating good karma that could carry into future lives.
Nagarjuna tells us that wealth that we cannot give or enjoy is just
a source of suffering:

Enjoying wealth will bring happiness in this life.
Giving wealth brings happiness in future lives.
Wealth that is wasted by neither being enjoyed nor given
Brings only suffering and no happiness.

Sakya Pandita, the greatest scholar of the Sakya school of
Tibetan Buddhism, declares:

The best of wealth is giving,
The best of happiness is happiness of the mind.

Strong emotional afflictions such as desire ensnare us in suffering. Craving and grasping lead us away from true peace of
mind. To loosen our attachments, it is wise to reflect deeply on
the transience of all appearances. Ngagi Wangpo says:

The wealth of this life is like the honey of bees.
Although they collect it, it will be enjoyed by others.
The gatherings of relatives and friends are like the meetings of
    guests,
Although they are together, they will go their separate ways.
Life is impermanent like dew on the tips of grass.
Although we are here, our disappearance will come soon.
The Lord of Death is like spies,
Day and night seeing an opportunity to get us.
The phenomena of this life are like being about to awaken
    from a dream:

They are transitory and momentary, and we will go, leaving
   them all.
The karmas of cause and effect, like our shadow,
Will always follow after us.
Therefore people with wise minds
Follow the path of liberation from this very day.

The *Udanavarga* says:

If you wish to have all the happiness,
Renounce all the desires [for happiness].
By renouncing all the desires,
You will enjoy the supreme happiness.
So long as you cling to desired objects,
No satisfaction will come to you.
So whoever, through wisdom, refrains from desire,
Enjoys satisfaction.

Of all the emotional afflictions, ignorance is the chief poison. Caught up in our struggles, we find it difficult to see our transient, suffering world for what it is and to realize our true nature and the great openness of all appearances. Wisdom lies in whatever small steps we can take in releasing our grasping at "self." Shantideva says:

So, whoever wants to pacify sufferings
Should develop wisdom.

The *Dharmapada* says:

When you realize with your wisdom
That all the phenomenal existents are without self,
You will not be hurt by suffering.
This is the perfect path.

# GLOSSARY ⮌

*absolute light:* According to Longchenpa (45a–49b), the five mind-body constituents of mundane conception are the five Buddha bodies in Buddhahood. The five emotional afflictions are the five primordial wisdoms, and the five physical elements are the five pure lights, and so forth. In Buddhahood, they are present in the nature of oneness or union, peace, and joy, but in the mundane mind, the mind and its objects are perceived, grasped, and experienced as the five mind-body constituents, five emotional afflictions, and five physical elements, and so forth, in a dualistic, emotional, and suffering manner.

AH: According to Mahayana scriptures, AH is the origin of all sounds, expressions, and letters; it is unborn, uncreated, unfabricated, and is openness, pure and natural. It does not convey any conceptual expressions, but manifests the primordial nature of oneness, the emptiness.

*bardo:* According to Buddhism, after you die there will be a *bardo,* a transitional period, after which you will take rebirth in another life. In the *bardo,* if you are equipped, you can realize the ultimate nature and all the appearances can arise as oneness. *See* Tsele (45–64) and Sogyal Rinpoche (274–286).

*Buddha-bodies:* The different aspects of the Buddha. Most of the teachings present three Buddha-bodies. The ultimate-body is the total emptiness or openness aspect of Buddhahood. The enjoyment-body is the true or pure form of the Buddha. In this, all the appearances of Buddhas and the phenomenal appearances of the pure land are changeless and inseparable from Buddhahood itself. The manifestative body is not a true or pure Buddha-body. It is a form manifested for the ordinary beings to serve them according to their needs and perceptions.

*esoteric breathing practices:* In Tibetan Buddhism there are many esoteric (tantric) trainings of energy or air, such as the trainings of Lung *(rLung)* or Tsalung *(rTsa rLung)*. They employ the energies of the body as a powerful means to generate energy, which in turn brings the realization of the union of great bliss and openness, the ultimate truth. As the result, esoteric trainees live with inner heat without need of clothing to keep warm, fly in the sky like birds, sustain themselves on energy instead of gross food, and enjoy youthfulness and longevity. Also, one of the best ways of anchoring your energies and mind is to focus them at a designated point below the navel. Explanations of such trainings should be read in other books.

*five colors:* Each color has its own unique power of healing. Kun-khyen Longchenpa writes (I.331b/2): "As the wisdom [the true nature] is changeless, its lights appear in the color green. As the wisdom is pure, its lights appear white. As the wisdom embodies qualities, its lights appear yellow. As the wisdom embodies power, its lights appear red. As the wisdom accomplishes all the [four] actions, its lights appear blue."

He writes (II.21b/2): *Rang Shar* interprets: "The light of white color is [the light of action or energy] of peace; the light of yellow color is of development; the light of red color is of power [that brings all under control]; the light of green color is of force [that liberates the negatives]; and the light of blue color is the accomplishment of all the [four] actions."

*grasping at "self":* The concept of apprehending oneself ("I" and "my"), or other beings or things ("he" or "she," "this" or "that"), as if they were truly existing entities.

*light:* Ordinary lights such as daylight are characterized as the pure aspect of the gross elements: Natsok Rangtrol (130a/3): "The pure [aspect] of the gross elements is the light rays, such as the lights and rays of the sun and light rays of a crystal."

*light body:* Many accomplished Dzogchen masters of Tibet, at the time of their deaths, attain "light body" or "rainbow body" *(jalü)*, in which they dissolve their mortal bodies into pure light bodies and leave only their nails and hair behind. Some attain the "pure light body of great transference" *(jalü phowa chenpo)*, in which they transform their gross bodies into pure light bodies, without leaving behind any physical remnants at all. *See* Longchen Rabjam (137).

*lotus posture:* This is one of the most popular Eastern meditative postures. It consists of (a) sitting in full crossed-legged or lotus posture, (b) placing the hands on one's lap in the meditative gesture, (c) keeping the spine straight, (d) bending the neck by lowering the chin slightly, (e) stretching out the arms like wings or a yoke, (f) lowering the focus of the eyes to a yard or two in front of oneself, at the level of the tip of the nose, and (g) placing the tip of the tongue so that it touches the upper palate.

*mantra:* A powerful esoteric word or phrase or phrases in Sanskrit, which embodies the absolute nature of sound, speech, expression, and power. It is also the expression or manifestation of the quintessential wisdom and power of a divinity, a Buddha, or the Buddha. For a trainee, it can be recited as a meditation, prayer, or means of spiritual expression or action.

*Mantra of Guru Rinpoche*

| | |
|---|---|
| OM: | Seed syllable of Buddha Body |
| AH: | Seed syllable of Buddha Speech |
| HUM: | Seed syllable of Buddha Mind |
| VAJRA: | Diamond (adamantine), Dharmakaya (absolute nature of the Buddha) |
| GURU: | Master (prosperity), Sambhogakaya (pure form of the Buddha) |
| PADMA: | Lotus (pureness), Nirmanakaya (Buddha body perceived by ordinary beings) |
| SIDDI: | Attainments of common and uncommon results |
| HUM: | Please grant; May it be. (Supplication) |

*Mantra of the Buddha of Compassion:* In Buddhist canonical texts, the mantra has only six syllables, but in most of the discovered *(terma)* texts, it has seven syllables with HRI, which is the heart syllable of Avalokiteshvara. In this mantra, HRI is the Buddha's heart syllable to be invoked, and the other six syllables are the means to invoke it.

| | |
|---|---|
| OM: | A + O + M = OM; symbolizes the body, speech, and mind of the Buddhas, which are embodied by Avalokiteshvara. |
| MANI: | Jewel; symbolizes the fulfillment of wishes, the skillful means. |
| PADME: | Lotus; symbolizes the undefiled purity, wisdom. The training on skillful means and wisdom is the Buddhist spiritual path, and their perfection is the skillful means and wisdom of Buddhahood. |
| HUNG: | Union, invoking, or uniting. It represents the union of skillful means and wisdom. It invokes the Buddha to bestow skillful means and wisdom and all the blessings. Alternatively, HUNG unites one inseparably with the (Body, Speech, and Mind of the) Buddha. |

HRI:   Heart syllable; represents the heart essence of the Buddha of compassion to be invoked and to be united with.

Simple meaning: "O Buddha who holds jewel and lotus [compassion and wisdom], please bestow your blessings upon us."

OM AH HUNG *breathing:* OM is the changeless strength and beauty of the true nature we all possess, the Buddha-body. AH is the ceaseless expression and prevailing energy of reality, the Buddha-speech. HUNG is the unmoving perfection of reality's primordial openness, the Buddha-mind. There are also practices in which one exhales with OM, inhales with HUNG, and holds the breath with AH, or exhales with OM, inhales with AH, and holds with HUNG. See Dilgo Khyentse (71a/6).

*pure land:* The Buddha forms and the phenomenal appearances of the land where Buddhas remain. In Buddhahood, there are no objective and subjective distinctions. All are present in the state of oneness, as the wisdom and the power of the wisdom with peace, joy, and beauty. This term has also been translated as Buddha-land or Buddha-field.

*terma:* Teachings and objects discovered through enlightened power. *See* Tulku Thondup Rinpoche.

*true nature:* It is also termed Buddha-nature, ultimate nature, absolute truth, enlightened nature, or Buddha Mind.

*tsa ba and grang ba:* According to Tibetan medicine, all physical sicknesses are related to either *tsa ba* (hot) or *grang ba* (cold) temperature. The upper body is the center of *tsa ba*, and the lower body is the center of *grang ba*.

*ultimate sphere (Dharmadhatu):* Shakya Chokden writes (306/5): "The ultimate sphere [ultimate space] is the wisdom of the Buddha that pervades the basis, path and result." He writes (307/5) that ultimate sphere can also be explained in three contexts: "In the context of the basis, samsara, the ultimate sphere is present as the absolute pure nature. In the context of the path, in the noble ones or highly attained sages of the Mahayana, it is present as the developing [or realizing] aspect of the Dharmakaya with two purities [purity from suddenly arising defilements and purity in its true nature from primordial time]. In the context of result, the Buddha Stage, it is present as the spontaneously accomplished three Buddha-bodies and Buddha-actions."

*vajra ("diamond")*: Symbolizes the adamantine, indestructible, and unchanging quality. Like the cross in Christianity, it is the main spiritual emblem of esoteric Buddhism. The vajra is also like a scepter, an implement held by deities or used in ceremonies, representing the masculine power.

# BIBLIOGRAPHY
## WORKS CITED WITH
## KEY TO ABBREVIATIONS ⌁

ASANGA: *Theg Pa Ch'en Po rGyud Bla Ma* by Asanga. Vol. PHI (ff. 54a–73a), Sems Tsam, Tenjur. Dege edition, Tibet.

ATISHA: *Byang Ch'ub Sems dPa'i Nor Bu'i Phreng Ba* by Dipamkarashrijnana [Atisha, 982–1054]. Vol. KHI (ff. 294b/7–295a/1), dBu Ma, Tenjur. Dege edition.

AVATAMSAKA-SUTRA: *sPyod Yul Yongs Su Dag Pa*. Chap. 16 (ff. 210b/2–219b/5, vol. KA) of *Sangs rGyas Phal Bo Ch'e* (Skt., *Avatamsaka-sutra*), Kajur. Dege edition.

BERNIE SIEGEL: *Love, Medicine, and Miracles* by Bernie S. Siegel, M.D. (Harper Perennial, 1990).

BHADRACHARYA-PRANIDHANA: *'Phags Pa bZang Po sPyod Pa'i sMon Lam Gyi rGyal Po* (Skt., *Bhadracharya-pranidhana-raja*). Vol. WAM, gZungs 'Dus, Kajur. Dege edition.

BIBLE: *The New Jerusalem Bible* (Doubleday & Company, 1985).

BILL MOYERS: *Healing and the Mind* by Bill Moyers (Doubleday, 1993).

CHANDRAKIRTI: *dBu Ma La 'Jug Pa* by Chandrakirti. Vol. A' (ff. 201a–219a), dBu Ma, Tenjur. Dege edition.

CHIM JAMPEYANG: *Ch'os mNgon Pa'i mDzod Kyi Tshig Leur Byas Pa'i 'Grel Ba mNgon Pa'i rGyan* (f. 430) by Chim Jampeyang [mCh'ims Ch'en] (Sadu Gyurme, India).

DHARMAPADA: *Dharmapada*. (A Theravadin canonical scripture)

Translated into Tibetan by Gedun Chöphel (1905–1951). mKhas dBang dGe 'dun Ch'os 'Phel Kyi gSung rTsom Phyogs sGrigs, pp. 253–340 (Sichuan Mirig Petrun Khang, China).

DHARMASAMGITI: *'Phags Pa Ch'os Yang Dag Par sDud Pa* (Skt., *Dharmasamgiti*). Vol. ZHA (ff. 1a–99b), mDo sDe, Kajur. Dege edition.

DILGO KHYENTSE: *dPal Ch'en 'Dus Pa'i Las Byang Gi dGongs Don Chung Zad bShad Pa Zab Don gSal Byed Rin Ch'en sNang Ba* by Jigme Khyentse Ozer [Dilgo Khyentse, 1910–1991] (Chöten Gonpa, Sikkim, India).

DODRUPCHEN: *sKyid sDug Lam 'Khyer Gyi Man Ngag* by Jigme Tenpe Nyima (1865–1926). Vol. KHA (ff. 475–491), Collection of Third Dodrupchen's Writings. (Lama Sangye, India). English translation: See below, *Enlightened Living*, pp. 117–130.

DO KHYENTSE: *Yang gSang Thugs Kyi Ch'a Lag Las bSang Khrus Zhi Ba Lha Ch'ab* (f. 3) by Do Khyentse Yeshe Dorje (1800–1866) (Dodrupchen Rinpoche, Sikkim, India).

DRI-ME ÖZER: *Sems Nyid Ngal gSo'i dGe Ba gSum Gyi Don Khrid Byang Ch'ub Lam bZang* (f. 53) by Dri-me Özer [Longchen Rabjam, 1308–1363] (Dodrupchen Rinpoche, India).

ENLIGHTENED LIVING: *Enlightened Living*, translated by Tulku Thondup, edited by Harold Talbott. (Shambhala Publications, 1990).

FIRST DALAI LAMA: *'Dul Ba'i Gleng gZhi Rin Po Ch'e'i mDzod* (f. 561) by Gedundrub, the First Dalai Lama (1391–1474) (Nechung & Lhakhar, India, 1970).

HAIVAJRA: *Kyai rDo rJe Zhes Bya Ba rGyud Kyi rGyal Po* (Skt., *Haivajra*). Vol. NGA (ff. 1a–29a), Gyud. Dege edition.

HERBERT BENSON: *Beyond the Relaxation Response* by Herbert Benson, M.D. (Berkeley Books, 1985).

JIGME GYALWE NYUGU: *'Gro mGon Bla Ma Rin Po Ch'e'i sPyi'i mNgon rTogs rGyal Sras Lam bZang* [An Autobiography of Jigme Gyalwe Nyugu, 1765–1843]. Photocopy provided by Tulku Pema Wangyal Rinpoche. See English summary under *Tulku Thondup* below.

JIGME LINGPA: *Rang Byung rDo rJe'i rNam Par Thar Pa Legs Byas Yong 'Dus sNye Ma* (f. 251) (An Autobiography of Jigme Lingpa). Vol. TA, Jigling Kabum (Dodrupchen Rinpoche, India). See English summary under *Tulku Thondup* below.

KARMA CHAKME: *Ri Ch'os mTshams Kyi Zhal gDams* (f. 299) by Karma Chakme (1613?–1678?) (Trashi Jong, India).

KHENPO NGACHUNG: *Padma Las 'Brel rTsal Gyi rTogs Pa brJod Pa Ngo mTshar sGyu Ma'i Rol Gar* (f. 147) (An Autobiography of Khenpo Ngachung, 1879–1941) (Sonam T. Kazi, India, 1969). See English summary under *Tulku Thondup* below.

KHYENTSE WANGPO: *Tshe dBang mDa' 'Phel Ma'i Ch'og bsGirgs 'Ch'i Med 'Byung Ba* (f. 23) by Khyentse Wangpo (1820–1892). Vol. DZA, Rinchen Terdzö (Dilgo Khyentse Rinpoche, India).

KUNKHYEN LONGCHENPA: *Theg mCh'og Rin Po Ch'e'i mDzod* by Longchen Rabjam. Vols. 1 & 2 (Dodrupchen Rinpoche, India).

LALITAVISTARA: *'Phags Pa rGya Ch'er Rol Pa* [Skt., *Lalitavistara*). Vol. KHA (ff. 1a–216b), mDo sDe, Kajur. Dege edition.

LEO TOLSTOY: "The Three Questions" (pp. 82–88), from *Fables and Fairy Tales* by Leo Tolstoy, translated by Ann Dunnigan (New American Library, A Signet Classic).

LONGCHENPA: *Tshig Don Rin Po Ch'e'i mDzod* (f. 243) by Ngagi Wangpo (Longchen Rabjam) (Dodrupchen Rinpoche, India).

LONGCHEN RABJAM: *The Practice of Dzogchen* by Longchen Rabjam. Translated with Commentary by Tulku Thondup Rinpoche, edited by Harold Talbott (Snow Lion Publications, 1996).

LONGCHEN RABJAMPA: *Ch'os dBying Rin Po Ch'e'i mDzod* (f. 26) by Longchen Rabjam (Dodrupchen Rinpoche, India).

MIPHAM RINPOCHE: *Man Ngag Gud Du sBas Pa'i Upadesha Rin Po Ch'e'i Za Ma Tog*. A collection of writings by Longchen Rabjam, Paltrul, and Mipham. Manuscript.

NAGARJUNA: *Gyal Po La gTam Bya Ba Rin Po Ch'e'i Phreng Ba* by Nagarjuna (2nd century CE?). Vol. GE (ff. 107a/1–126a/4), sPring Yig, Tenjur. Dege edition.

NATSOK RANGTROL: *sNyan brGyud Kyi rGyab Ch'os Ch'en Mo Zab Don gNad Kyi Me Long* by Natsok Rangtrol (Longchen Rabjam). Vol. VAM (ff. 77a–247b), rGyab Ch'os of Zab Mo Yang Tig from Yazhi (Sherab G. Lama, Delhi, 1975).

NGAGI WANGPO: *Thur Pa La bsKul Ba'i Rabs* by Ngag Gi dBang Po (Longchen Rabjam). Vol. 1 (pp. 312–331), Sung Thorbu (Sangje Dorje, India, 1973).

NGAWANG PALZANG: *rDzogs Pa Ch'en Po Klong Ch'en sNying Thig Gi sNgon 'Gro'i Khrid Yig Kun bZang Bla Ma'i Zhal Lung Gi Zin Bris* (f. 205) by Ngawang Palzang (Khenpo Ngachung, 1879–1941). Xylograph print.

OMRAAM AÏVANHOV: *A New Earth* by Omraam Mikhaël Aïvanhov (Prosveta Editions, Frejus, 1982).

Paltrül Rinpoche: *rDzogs Pa Ch'en Po Klong Ch'en sNying Thig Gi sNgon 'Gro'i Khrid Yig Kun bZang Bla Ma'i Zhal Lung* (f. 307) by Ogyen Jigme Chökyi Wangpo (Paltrül Rinpoche, 1808–1887) (Ponlob Rinpoche, Sikkim, India).

Rahula: *What the Buddha Taught* by Walpola Rahula (Grove Press, 1980).

Raymond Moody: *The Light Beyond* by Raymond A. Moody, Jr. (Bantam Books, 1989).

Sakya Pandita: *Legs Par bShad Pa Rin Po Ch'e'i gTer Zhes Bya Ba'i bsTan bChos* (f. 39) by Kunga Gyaltsen (Sakya Pandita, 1181–1251). Xylograph print from Tibet.

Shakya Chokden: *Ch'os Kyi dByings Su bsTod-Pa'i rNam bShad Ch'os Kyi dByings rNam Par Nges Pa.* Vol. 7 (ff. 303–346), Collected Works of gSer mDog Pan Chen Shakya mCh'og lDan (1428–1507) (Kunzang Tobgey, India, 1975).

Shantideva: *Byang Ch'ub Sems dPa'i sPyod Pa La 'Jug Pa* (Skt., *Bodhi-caryavatara*) by Shantideva (8th century CE). Vol. LA (ff. 1a–40a), dBu Ma, Tenjur. Dege edition. English translations: *A Guide to the Bodhisattva's Way of Life* by Stephen Batchelor; *Entering the Path of Enlightenment* by Marion Matics; *Meaningful to Behold*, with commentary by Geshe Kelsang Gyatso.

Shedgyud: *bDud rTsi sNying Po Yan Lag brGyad Pa gSang Ba Man Ngag Gi rGyud Las Dum Bu gNyis Pa bShad Pa'i rGyud* (One of the Four Tantras on Medicine), discovered by Trawa Ngonshe (1012–1090?) (Smanrtsis sPendzod, Leh, India, 1978).

Sogyal Rinpoche: *The Tibetan Book of Living and Dying* by Sogyal Rinpoche (Harper Collins, 1992).

Tsele: *Mirror of Mindfulness, the Cycle of the Four Bardos* by Tsele Natsok Rangdrol, translated by Erik Pema Kunsang (Shambhala Publications, 1989).

Tsele Natsok Rangtrol: *Dri Lan sKal bZang dGa' Byed* (f. 81) by Gotsangpa [rTse Le] Natshog Rangtrol (1608–?). Xylograph print of Shri Neu sTeng, Tibet.

Tsewang Chokdrub: *gSang sNgags Nang Gi Lam Rim rGya Ch'er 'Grel Pa Sangs rGyas gNyis Pa'i dGongs rGyan* (f. 456) by Gyurme Tsewang Chokdrub (1764–?) (Smanrtsis Spendzod, Leh, India, 1972).

Tsongkhapa: *Byang Ch'ub Lam Rim Ch'e Ba* (f. 523) by Nyamme Tsongkhapa Chenpo (1357–1419) (Bud Med Tshogs Pa, Kalimpong, India).

Tsultrim Lodrö: *Yid bZhin Rin Po Ch'e'i mDzod* by Tsultrim Lodrö (Longchen Rabjam) (Dodrupchen Rinpoche, India).

Tulku Thondup: *Masters of Meditation and Miracles: The Longchen Nyingthig Lineage of Tibetan Buddhism* by Tulku Thondup (Shambhala Publications, 1996).

Tulku Thondup Rinpoche: *Hidden Teachings of Tibet* by Tulku Thondup Rinpoche, edited by Harold Talbott (Wisdom Publications, 1986).

Udanavarga: *Ch'ed Du brJod Pa'i Tshom* (Skt., *Udanavarga*). Vol. sa (ff. 209a–253b), mDo sDe, Kajur. Dege edition.

Upanishad: *Maitri-upanishad* 3.2, in *A Sourcebook in Indian Philosophy*, edited by Sarvepalli Radhakrishnan and Charles A. Moore (Princeton University Press, 1973).

Vasubandhu: *Ch'os mNgon Pa'i mDzod* by Vasubandhu (4th century CE?). Vol. ku (ff. 1a–25a), mNgon Pa, Tenjur. Dege edition.

Yukhok Chatralwa: *rDo rJe'i mGur dByanqs* (f. 19) by Chöying Rangtrol (Yukhok Chatralwa, 1872–1950). Manuscript.

Zhabkarpa: *A'od gSal rDzogs Pa Ch'en Po'i Khregs Ch'od lTa Ba'i Klu dByangs Sa Lam Myur Du bGrod Pa'i rTsal lDan mKa' lDing gShog rLabs* (f. 35) by Tsogtrug Rangtrol (Zhabkarpa, 1781–1851) (Phuntsok Chökhorling, India).

Zurkharpa: *Mes Po'i Zhal Lung* (A Commentary on the Four Tantras of Medicine) by Zurkhar Lodrö Gyatso (1508–?), 4 vols. (Smanrtsis Spendzod, Leh, India, 1980).